Peter Bailey
1802 to 1880

The

PETER BAILEY
Family History

Beginning with Nickolas Bailey
Born 1755, Died 1831

Edited and Expanded
by
W.S.Chellberg
Wheaton, Illinois

Originally Titled:
History of the Bailey Family
The Committee
October 1922

The Peter Bailey Family History

Additional copies my be obtained from --

W.S.Chellberg

w.s.c@sbcglobal.net

or

LuLu Press

www.lulu.com

✶✶✶✶✶✶✶✶✶

Library of Congress Cataloging-in-Publication Data

Chellberg, W.S. William S., 1936-
  Peter Bailey Family History : Beginning with Nickolas Bailey, born
1755, died 1831 / edited and expanded by W.S.Chellberg
      p. cm.
Rev. ed. of: History of the Bailey Family. 1922.
Includes bibliographical references and index.
    ISBN 0-912868-04-X (pbk. : alk. paper)
1. Bailey family. 2. Bailey, Nickolas, 1755-1831 -- Family. I. title.
    CS71.B152003
    929'.2'0973--dc22   2003022405

✶✶✶✶✶✶✶✶✶

CONTENTS

Generation 1 11

Generation 2 15

Generation 3 19

Generation 4 27

Generation 5 47

Generation 6 71

Generation 7 81

Generation 8 89

Index of Names 93

Family Notes 120

****

COVER PHOTOS:

Front --- Clockwise from upper right: Peter Bailey; the Third Grade Class Photo of J.W.Bailey; Dr. Alvin L. Bailey.

Back --- Top: Bailey Coat of Arms. Center: Wife of Absalom Bailey - Cassie C. (Leffler) Bailey.

REPORT OF THE ORIGINAL EDITORIAL COMMITTEE

In submitting this family record of the Peter Bailey family, we have no apology to offer. We have done our best in obtaining the data; we had a very tedious, long-drawn effort. Some members of the family resided in distant states, their addresses unknown to us; some we have never heard of. We had to depend upon the assistance of others very materially. Some refused to send in data or only part, requiring, frequently, a voluminous correspondence.

Mistakes will and have crept in by carelessness in copy of family Bible, etc; so we had to depend upon our own reason in many cases, judging out facts the best we could. So if mistakes have crept in with all our vigilance and care, we have done our best to prevent it.

We wish to thank one and all who have so assisted us in any way in this work.

The Committee,
Marion Bailey, Lizton, Indiana
Alvin L. Bailey, Chesaning, Michigan
October, 1922

Editorial Notes

This book, *The PETER BAILEY Family History*, truly was a monumental undertaking for the above named 'Committee' when we consider they were working with only the typewriter and the pen. Using the electronic conveniences that we have today it considerably simplifies this work.

We must remember that very little of what we call documentation was done in the preparation of this work. To be a proper genealogy each name, date, place, and relationship must be documented. That work is left to you and I, and any future generations that are interested.

I have completely set this book in new, more readable type, and have attempted to make it easier to follow in structure. I have numbered each generation with the following symbol - **<5>**, and have put a bullet (•) before each child's name. Following the name of each person there is a page number to reference that person's siblings or parents; (e.g. James W. Bailey, **[p. 25]**). I have restrained myself from doing much editing in the sense of removing or altering little inserted comments, such as, "… and his splendid wife …". I have placed a headline above each section dealing with each one of Peter Bailey's children and their offspring. I, also, have updated the work as much as possible following my branch of the tree, which is: Peter Bailey>Absalom Bailey>James W. Bailey>Irene G. (Bailey) Chellberg.

I hope you find the new structure more readable and helpful in building your own family tree. It may be as documentation is done and new branches are added that this work will be re-published. I hope what I have done is a beginning.

W.S. Chellberg
July 2003
Revised: 2021

THE FIRST OF THE NAME OF BAILEY

Very few names have been so long and extensively used as a surname. In Scotland it is one of the oldest names there; and in the North and scattered throughout England and the North of Ireland.

Benoni Bailey was one of the early settlers of Danbury, Conn., whence descendents settled in Philadelphia.

Guido Bailey was a proprietor of Salem in 1642; and was a juror at Bridgewater in 1658-59. Henry Bailey lived in Salem in 1638-47.

James Bailey was a proprietor of Rowley in 1642; and was fifty-one years old in 1663. He died in 1677 and left two sons, John and James Bailey.

John Bailey was a weaver and proprietor of Salisbury in 1639; and died in Newbury in 1651. He left sons, John and Joseph.

In 1635 Richard Bailey, fifteen years of age, came in the "Bevis". He settled at Newbury, removed to Rowley; and died in 1647. His son, Joseph, was mentioned in his will.

Thomas Bailey was a town officer of Weymouth in 1645. He died in 1681: and his will mentions his sons, John and Thomas Bailey.

GENERATION 1

Nickolas Bailey

<1> **NICKOLAS (Nicholas) BAILEY**, the father of Peter Bailey, who is the grandfather of this great family of the oldest living generation who are the grandfathers and grandmothers of today, was born in Baker County, Pennsylvania, September 25, 1755. This is as far back in our record that is obtainable.

He was united in marriage to Susanna Leffler, his second wife, December 1, 1799 in Northumberland County, Pennsylvania. She was born December 31, 1776, in this same county. We have no record of his first marriage. Four sons and five daughters were born to this union, viz.:

- Peter Bailey, the oldest son and grandfather of our family was born in Northumberland County, Pennsylvania, in 1802.
- Jacob Bailey in Crawford County, Pennsylvania, in 1803.
- Elizabeth Bailey in Crawford County, Pennsylvania, in 1806.
- John Bailey in Crawford County, Pennsylvania, in 1807.
- Lidia Bailey in Crawford County in 1809.
- Nancy Bailey, December 11, 1811.
- Philip Bailey, September 13, 1813.
- Barbary Bailey, March 30,1816.
- Molly Bailey, June 12, 1818.

The family must have immigrated to Butler County, Ohio where Nickolas, the father, died March 14, 1831, at the age of 76 years, 5 months and 14 days. Susanna, the mother, died September 6, 1859, in Butler County, Ohio; age 82 years, 8 months and 6 days.

GENERATION 2

Children of Nickolas Bailey <2>

This record was taken from the family Bible of Peter Bailey.

We have no record of what became of the rest of the family, viz.: — Jacob Bailey, Lidia Bailey, Nancy Bailey, Phillip Bailey, Barbary Bailey and Molly Bailey, except John Bailey who in the memory of some now living made a visit to his brother Peter in St. Paul, Indiana, about 50 years ago. He then resided in Eaton, Preble County, Ohio, and no doubt died there. It was said that he had one daughter; we have no record of it.

<2> **Peter Bailey,** [p.13] the grandfather of our family was born in Northumberland County, Pennsylvania, March 6, 1802. He was united in marriage to Elizabeth Stanbrook, April 4, 1822, at the age of twenty years. His wife was born October 4, 1803. Thirteen children were born to this union.

- Nicholas Bailey (2) was born in Butler County, Ohio, November 10, 1822
- Susan Bailey in Butler County, Ohio, June 23, 1824
- Catherine Bailey born July 16, 1826, she died November 29, 1826.
- John Bailey (2) in Butler County, September 19, 1827
- Mary Ann Bailey, in Butler County, Ohio, August 31, 1829
- Peter J. Bailey in Butler County, Ohio, September 19, 1831
- Elizabeth Bailey (2) in Butler County, Ohio, July 16, 1833
- Lidia Bailey (2) in Shelby County, Indiana, September 5, 1835
- Isaac and Abraham Bailey (twins) in Shelby County, Indiana, July 8, 1838. These children died in infancy. Isaac died December 1868. Abraham, April 6, 1838.
- Henry Bailey in Shelby County, Indiana, February 20, 1841
- Absalom Bailey in Shelby County, Indiana, October 19, 1844
- Marthia Bailey in Shelby County, Indiana, June 19, 1847. She died June 28, 1847, age 9 days.

Peter Bailey <2> moved to Shelby County, Indiana from Ohio with his family some time between 1833 and 1835. He obtained land from the Government, the farm now owned by Hasson Bailey and James Bailey with the old mill now gone owned by Wright Bailey. The mill was washed away March 23, 1897. It was known as the old Bailey Mill. His wife Elizabeth died June 22, 1847, three days after the birth of the last child.

Peter Bailey was again united in marriage to a widow by the name of Martha Collier sometime in 1847. She was born December 28, 1810. Two children were born to this union, viz.:

- George Bailey, born October 14, 1848.
- Solome Bailey, September 18, 1850.

His second wife died March 1, 1876; age 65 years, 2 months and 3 days. He died December 16, 1880, aged 78 years, 9 months and 11 days. This man we are proud to know was one of the leading citizens of his time.

<2> **Elizabeth Bailey,** [p. 13] daughter of Nickolas Bailey, married a man by the name of Jacob Reed and there were three sons and three daughters born to this union all we Lave any record of, viz.: —

- Dan Reed
- Lidia Reed
- Eliza Reed
- Jake Reed
- Mary Reed
- Conrad Reed.

GENERATION 3

Children of Peter Bailey <3>

Son of Nickolas and Susanna Bailey

<3> **Nicholas Bailey (2)**, [p. 17] the oldest son of Peter Bailey, was born in Butler County, Ohio, November 10, 1822, he was united in marriage to Sarah Ann (N.?) Isley, November 20, 1845, in Decater County, Indiana. To this union was born five children, viz.: —

- Elizabeth (3) Bailey, born September 3, 1846, in Shelby County, Indiana.
- American Ann Bailey, on March 15, 1849, Shelby County, Indiana.
- An infant, December 5, 1850, Shelby County, Indiana.
- Katie Ann (Katia?) Bailey, April 20, 1852, Shelby County, Indiana.
- John P. Bailey, May 30, 1856, Shelby County, Indiana.

His wife died May 30, 1857, Shelby County, Indiana, age 33 years, 7 months and 14 days. Her death was evidently the result of childbirth.

Nicholas Bailey (2), <3> married the second time to a widow, Mary Ellen Creed Halterman, October 19, 1858, in Rush County, Indiana. Wife born October 19, 1831—Died August 31, 1914. To this union were born seven children, viz.: —

- Joseph Wright Bailey in Shelby County, Indiana, August 6, 1869.
- Laura Bailey in Shelby County. Indiana, February 5, 1862.
- Fernando Wood Bailey in Shelby County, Indiana, October 23, 1863.
- Nellie Bailey in Shelby County, Indiana August 1, 1867.
- Van P. Bailey in Shelby County, Indiana, March 11, 1869.
- Warren D. Bailey in Shelby County, Indiana June 12, 1873.
- James Curtis Bailey in Shelby County, Indiana September 8, 1875.

<3> **Susan Bailey**, [p. 17] the oldest daughter and second child of Peter and Elizabeth Bailey, was born June 23, 1824,

in Butler County, Ohio. She was united in marriage to Rossell J. Pearce at the age of 20 years, August 29, 1844, in Shelby County, Indiana. To this union were born eight children, viz.: —

- Eliza Jane Pearce was born in Decatur County, Indiana, August 6, 1846.
- William A. Pearce was born in Decatur County, Indiana, August 11, 1848.
- Mary Edna Pearce was born in Decatur County, Indiana, December 12, 1850.
- John Willis Pearce was born in Decatur County, Indiana, October 10, 1852.
- Charles M. Pearce was born in Decatur County, Indiana, February 1, 1856.
- George Thomas Pearce was born in Decatur County, Indiana, April 27, 1858.
- Amanda Alice Pearce was born in Boone County, Indiana, December 21, 1864.
- Ornetta L. Pearce was born in Boone, County, Indiana, and September 28, 1866.

William Pearce was married the second time to Minerva Campbell, February 25, 1915, at Horton, Kansas, his present address.

<3> **John Bailey (2)**, [p. 17] second son and fourth child of Peter and Elizabeth Bailey was born in Butler County, Ohio, September 19, 1827. He was united in marriage to Catherine Emday, the stepdaughter of Edward Kurr, October 23, 1847. To this union were born four children, viz.: —

- Elizabeth (4) Bailey was born in Shelby County, Indiana, April 19, 1849.
- Sarah Bailey was born April 24, 1851. Died September 19, 1852.
- Eva Ann Bailey was born March 8, 1853.
- Marion Bailey, the only son, was born in Shelby County, Indiana, December 1, 1854.

John Bailey <3> was married the second time to Rebecca J. Reed, July 2, 1856. John Bailey died August 7, 1902. Rebecca

J. died February 6, 1913. To this union were born ten children, viz.: —

- Infant, born March 30, 1857. Died March 30, 1857.
- Mary M. Bailey, born June 12, 1858.
- George W. Bailey, born October 2, 1860.
- Peter N. Bailey, born November 26, 1862.
- Susan E. Bailey, born January 21, 1865.
- Willie Bailey, born February 9, 1867. Died November 4, 1867
- Nettie Bailey, born October 11, 1868.
- Nora Bailey, born May 8, 1872.
- Edgar S. Bailey, born February 21, 1877.
- John T. Bailey, born January 20, 1887.

<3> **Mary Ann Bailey,** [p. 17] the fifth child and third daughter of Peter and Elizabeth Bailey was united in marriage to Absalom McCain, July 4, 1847. The mother died in St. Paul, Indiana, December 1, 1856. To this union were born five children, viz. –

- William Solomon McCain, born August 3, 1848.
- Margarette Elizabeth McCain, born April 5, 1850.
- George Washington McCain, born October 2, 1852.
- Sabina Jane McCain, born January 25, 1854.
- John Franklin McCain, born May 16, 1855.

<3> **Peter J. Bailey**, [p. 17] third son and sixth child of Peter Bailey was born September 19, 1831. He was united in marriage to Phoebe Ann Feaster in St. Paul, Indiana, February 21, 1858. Peter Bailey died in St. Paul, Indiana, December 24, 1884. Age 53 years, 3 months and 5 days. Phoebe, his wife, died April 5, 1919. She was born August 1, 1840. Her age at death was 78 years, 6 months and 4 days. Three children were

born to this union, viz.: —

- Alvin L. Bailey, August 12, 1859.
- Daniel V. Bailey, May 26, 1862.
- Louis A. Bailey, February 20, 1864.

<3> **Elizabeth (2) Bailey**, [p. 17] fourth daughter and seventh child of Peter and Elizabeth Bailey was united in marriage to Joseph Henderson in St. Paul, Indiana. To this union one living child was born, viz.: —

- Lucinda Henderson, born February 10, 1853.

<3> **Lidia Bailey (2)**, [p. 17] eighth child and fifth daughter of Peter and Elizabeth Bailey was united in marriage to Thomas Roebuck. Thomas J. Roebuck, the father, died February 29, 1888. The family moved to Elk City, Kansas in June, 1882, where they have resided and in Oklahoma since. To this union were born thirteen children, viz.:—

- An infant daughter, born June 6, 1857. Died June 6, 1857.
- An infant daughter, born June 6, 1857, Died June 6, 1857.
- Derias P. Roebuck, born November 27, 1858.
- Charles F. Roebuck, born July 1, 1862. Died February 15, 1864.
- George B. McCleen Roebuck, born November 14, 1863. Died November 28, 1889.
- John H. N. Roebuck, born October 29, 1865. Died April 5, 1919.
- Robert E. L. Roebuck, born November 26, 1867. Died September 16, 1868.
- Hiram A. Roebuck, born February 26, 1869. Died March 18, 1869.
- Emma L. Roebuck, born March 20, 1870.
- Thomas Benton Roebuck, born June 1, 1872.
- Mary E. Roebuck, born November 16, 1874.
- Frances M. Roebuck, born May 17, 1876.
- Lillie Roebuck, born February 17, 1888.

<3> **Henry Bailey**, [p. 17] the eleventh child and sixth son of Peter and Elizabeth Bailey, was born February 20, 1841. He was united in marriage to Amanda A. Creed, October 27, 1866. Amanda was born May 12, 1845. Died July 15, 1920. One child was born to this union, viz.:--

- Hasson E. Bailey, May 17, 1868.

<3> **Absalom Bailey**, [p. 17] the seventh son and twelfth child of Peter and Elizabeth Bailey, was born October 19, 1844. He was united in marriage to C. Cassie Leffler, January 13, 1867. C. Cassie Bailey died June 10, 1894. To this union were born seven children, viz.:—

- John H. Bailey, February 25, 1868. Died March 24, 1869.
- Mary E. Bailey, September 9, 1870. Died November 24, 1872.
- Charles C. Bailey, February 17, 1872. Died December 10, 1959.
- Dessie M. Bailey, January 12, 1874. Died May 8, 1958.
- James W. Bailey, September 20, 1876. Died February 28, 1925.
- Minnie B. Bailey, December 12, 1878. Died July 30, 1880.
- Lola G. Bailey. June 23, 1883.

Absalom Bailey <3> was married the second time, to Elizabeth Hall Martin, March 26, 1896. His second wife died February 7, 1920. Absalom Bailey died June 24, 1904, age 60 years, 9 months and 5 days.

Children of Peter and Martha Bailey, his second wife.

<3> **George Bailey**, [p. 18] first child of Peter Bailey and Martha Bailey, was born October 14, 1848. He was married to Sarah A. Townsend, October 11, 1870. Sarah was born September 19, 1852. George departed this life July 19, 1913.

<3> **Salome Bailey**, [p. 18] second child of Peter Bailey

and Martha Bailey, was born in St. Paul, Indiana, September 8, 1850. She was married to Samuel Crumrine, January, 1872. She died November 29, 1912, in Los Angeles, California. No children.

Children of Elizabeth (Bailey) Reed <3>

Daughter of Nickolas and Susanna Bailey

<3> **Lidia Reed**, [p. 18] daughter of Elizabeth Reed, married a man by the name of Favor. The Mother and Father departed this life some years ago. We regret very much that more was not be obtainable of the rest of the family. To this union was born, viz.:—

- Frances Favor
- Peter Favor
- William Favor
- John Favor
- Jake Favor

<3> **Eliza Reed**, [p. 18] daughter of Elizabeth Reed, married a man by the name of Benjamin Mason. The husband and wife departed this life some years ago. To this union was born, viz.:—

- John Mason
- William Mason
- Sarah Mason
- Ben Mason

GENERATION 4

Children of Nicholas Bailey (2) <4>
Son of Peter and Elizabeth Bailey

<4> **Elizabeth (3) Bailey**, [p. 21] the oldest child of Nicholas and Sara Ann Bailey was united in marriage to George Britton in St. Paul, Ind., September 9, 1860. Four children were born to this union, viz.:—

- Sadie E. Britton, October 9, 1862.
- Mahala A. Britton, December 12, 1863.
- Georgia Britton, July 20, 1872. He died in two weeks.
- Art Britton, born September 24, 1874, in Tipton County, Indiana.

<4> **American Ann Bailey**, [p. 21] second child of Nicholas and Sara Ann Bailey was married to Dave Widner at St. Paul, Indiana, about 1876. No children were born to this union. He died 1906. She died 1907.

<4> **Katie Ann Bailey**, [p. 21]fourth child of Nicholas and Sarah Ann Bailey was married to Benjamin Tucker in Shelby County, Indiana. Date: ?? To this union were born three children, viz.:—

- William Tucker, in 1872.
- Molly Tucker, in 1874.
- Ebert Tucker, in 1876. She died in 1876.

<4> **John P. Bailey**, [p. 21] fifth child and only son of Nicholas and Sara Ann Bailey, was married to Margaret C. Eckert, January 15, 1883. He died November 27, 1893. Margaret C.,

born January 26, 1860. Three children were born to this union, viz.:—

- Heail R. Bailey was born October 25, 1883.
- Sarah E. Bailey was born February 9, 1885.
- Jefferson D. Bailey was born July 28, 1888.

Children of Nicholas and Mary Ellen Creed Bailey <4>
Son of Peter and Elizabeth Bailey

<4> **Joseph Wright Bailey**, [p. 21] oldest child of Nicholas and Mary Ellen Bailey was married to Fannie Tevis, July 13, 1882. Mr. and Mrs. Wright Bailey reside in St. Paul, Indiana. Three children were born to this union, viz.:—

- Golda Alice Bailey, born May 12, 1883. She died September 4, 1915.
- James Oday Bailey, born December 29, 1887.
- Edith E. Bailey, born August 15, 1891.

<4> **Laura Bailey**, [p. 21] second child of Nicholas and Mary Ellen Bailey, was united in marriage to David F. Templeton, October 16, 1879. David F. Templeton, born March 31, 1856. To this union one daughter was born, viz.:—

- Leona M. Templeton, as born May 25, 1881.

<4> **Fernando Wood Bailey**, [p. 21] second son and third child of Nicholas and Mary Ellen Bailey was married to Nannie Templeton, November 6, 1882. Nannie departed this life May 4, 1913. To this union four children were born, viz.—

- Walter Bailey, born August 8, 1886
- Lena G. Bailey, born August 26, 1891.
- Fred Bailey, born July 10, 1893
- Loyd D. Bailey, born October 4, 1895.

Fernando Wood Bailey <4> was married the second time to Mrs. Ella C. Redenbough, February 24, 1915. No children. Mr. and Mrs. Fernando Bailey reside in Waldron, Shelby County, Indiana.

<4> **Nellie Bailey**, [p. 21] second daughter and fourth child of Nicholas and Ellen Bailey was married to A. E. Smith, October 5, 1885. Nellie Bailey departed this life August 19, 1906. Mr. Smith has remarried and will reside in St. Paul, Indiana. To this union were born 4 children, viz.:—

- Oral N. Smith, November 10, 1885.
- Forest E. Smith, October 17, 1890
- Mary A. Smith, July 6, 1897
- William E. Smith, November 11, 1902

<4> **Van P. Bailey**, [p. 21] the third son and fifth child of Nicholas and Ellen Bailey was united in marriage to Sarah P. Reed December 23, 1888. Mr. and Mrs. Van Bailey reside in Wannemaker, Indiana. Four children were born to this born, viz.:—

- Frank P. Bailey was born April 3, 1890.
- Mary Bailey was born October 5, 1893.
- Nicholas Bailey (3)was born September 22, 1899.
- Russell Bailey was born March 4, 1904.

<4> **Warren D. Bailey**, [p. 21] the fourth son and sixth child of Nicholas Bailey and Mary Ellen, was married to Lilly M. Righer, March 4, 1891. Lilly M. died June 13, 1910. To this union were born two children, viz.:—

- David Bailey. born December 8, 1893.
- Harry M. Bailey, born October 8, 1894. He died March 22, 1913.

Warren D. Bailey <4> was married a second time to Mary Kolkusler, December 25, 1910. No children. Mr. and Mrs. Warren Bailey reside on a farm near Waldron, Indiana.

<4> **James Curtis Bailey**, [p. 21] youngest child of Nicholas and Mary Ellen Bailey was united in marriage to Jesse Sweeney August 11, 1895. James C. Bailey resides in Indianapolis, Indiana. To this union were born three children, viz.:—

- George (2) Bailey, April 17, 1896.
- Grace Bailey, December 11, 1900
- Theodore Bailey, November 12, 1902. He died July 3, 1903.

Children of Susan (Bailey) Pearce <4>
Daughter of Peter and Elizabeth Bailey

<4> **Eliza Jane Pearce**, [p. 22] the oldest child, was married to Robert O. Watson, January 16, 1888. No children were born.

<4> **William A. Pearce**, [p. 22] the second child and oldest son of Rossell J. and Susan Pearce was married to Elizabeth Hall, December 31, 1868. Elizabeth, minister of the Church of Christ, the wife of William Pearce, died June 6, 1901. Ten children were born to this union, viz.:—

- Estelle F. Pearce, born in Hendricks County, Indiana, Feb. 7, 1871.
- Claud F. Pearce, born in Hendricks County, Indiana, May 17, 1872
- Charles D. Pearce, born in Hendricks County, Indiana, Jan. 22, 1874.
- Mary J. Pearce, born in Hendricks County, Indiana, Oct 30, 1875.
- Cecil V. Pearce, born in Hendricks County, Indiana, June 6, 1879.
- Maud P. Pearce, born in Boone County, Indiana, March 6, 1881.
- Dora A. Pearce, born in Hendricks County, Indiana, July 21, 1883.
- Morris F. Pearce, born in Coffey County, Kansas, March 6, 1885.
- Infant, born in Finney County, Kansas, 1888.
- Nellie D. Pearce, born in Finney County, Kansas, Jan. 12, 1891

<4> **Mary Edna Pearce**, [p. 22] third child and second daughter of Rossell and Susan Pearce was married to William

C. Woodard, January 14, 1867, in Boone County, Indiana. Four children were born to this union, viz.:—

- Viola May Woodard, August 1, 1868. Born in Indiana.
- Raymond Thurman Woodard, December 3, 1870. Born in Indiana.
- Nelly Ester Woodard, February 20, 1873. Born in Indiana.
- Irving Clyde Woodard, September 13, 1881. Born in Indiana.

<4> **John Willis Pearce**, [p. 22] second son and fourth child of Susan and Rossell Pearce was united in marriage to Ellen Deatley in Boone County, Indiana, September 6, 1877, and John died February 5, 1882. Two children were born to this union, viz.:—

- George Pearce
- Sarah Pearce.

John Willis' widow married and moved to Oregon and the balance of this record could not be secured.

<4> **Charles M. Pearce**, [p. 22] third son and fifth child of Susan Pearce, was married to Laura Pearcy, September 4, 1879, Boone County. Indiana. Charles M. Pearce, address Wetmore, Kansas. To this union two children were born, viz.: —

- Tessie Maud Pearce, born March 16, 1381, in Boone County, Indiana.
- William L. Pearce, born January 7, 1892, in Garfield County, Kansas.

<4> **George Thomas Pearce**, [p. 22] sixth child and fourth son of Susan and Rossell Pearce, was united in marriage to Lilly A. Dale, who was born in Boone County, Indiana, October 11, 1861. Married on September 6, 1880. To this marriage was born, viz.:—

- Arie Beaughn Pearce, born in Boone County, Indiana, February 18, 1882.
- Vera May Pearce, born in Boone County, Indiana, October 6, 1883.
- Vella Maude Pearce was born in Boone County, Indiana, November 6,

1885.

- Amy Leona Pearce was born in Finnly County, Kansas, July 21, 1889.

Children of John Bailey <4>
Son of Peter and Elizabeth Bailey

<4> **Elizabeth (4) Bailey**, [p. 22] the oldest child of Catherine and John Bailey was united in marriage to David Smith, March 4, 1869. David was born April 14, 1846. Died March 25, 1915. No children were born. Her address is Lizton, Indiana.

<4> **Eva Ann Bailey**, [p. 22] third child of Catherine and John Bailey was united in marriage to Martin Campbell, March 14, 1872. Martin Campbell was born March 10, 1848. To this union were born nine children, viz.:—

- Tessie O. Campbell, born in Vigo County, Indiana, March 10, 1873. Died June 12, 1895.
- Mary C. Campbell, born in Hendricks County, Indiana, February 15, 1875.
- Rosalee Campbell, born in Hendricks County, Indiana, June 20, 1876. Died October 16, 1876.
- John L. Campbell, born in Hendricks County, Indiana, September 5, 1877.
- Martin O. Campbell, born in Vigo County, Indiana, December 1, 1881.
- Oliver D. Campbell, born in Vigo County, Indiana, January 28, 1883.
- Sarah E. Campbell, born in Vigo County, Indiana, July 29, 1890.
- Eva A. Campbell, born in Vigo County, Indiana, May 16, 1892
- James M. Campbell, born in Vigo County, Indiana, September 29, 1895.

<4> **Marion Bailey**, [p. 22] the only son and fourth child of John and Catherine Bailey. His first wife (no name given) was

born December 1, 1854, in Shelby County, Indiana. He was united in marriage to Rachel C. Young, November 15, 1877, in Boone County, Indiana She was born December 27, 1855, in Montgomery County, Indiana. She died April 17, 1920. To this union were born five children, viz.:—

- An infant daughter still born May 25, 1881, in Hendricks County, Indiana.
- Harry E. Bailey, born December 23, 1882, in Hendricks County, Indiana.
- Artie M Bailey, born January 28, 1887, in Hendricks County, Indiana.
- Luna A Bailey, born June 14, 1888, in Hendricks County, Indiana.
- Goldie V. Bailey, born March 27, 1891, in Hendricks County, Indiana.

Children of John and Rebecca Bailey, his second wife.

<4> **Mary M. Bailey**, [p. 23] second oldest child of John and Rebecca Bailey, his second wife, was united in marriage to John H. Dale, November 12, 1873. To this union five children were born, viz.:—

- Lola D. Dale, October 22, 1875. Died February 14, 1876.
- Ira O. Dale, January 25, 1876.
- W. Edgar Dale was born October 31, 1879.
- An infant was born and died August 25, 1886.
- Charles B. Dale was born August 31, 1887.

<4> **George W. Bailey**, [p. 23] second child and oldest son of John and Rebecca Bailey, second wife, was born in Shelby County, Indiana, October 2, 1860. He was married to Hattie F. Vest, October 1, 1885. She died September 18, 1907. Eight children were born to this union, viz.:—

- Fannie J. Bailey, July 24, 1886, Boone County, Indiana.
- Olga Jesse Bailey, was born in Hendricks County, Indiana, September 2, 1887. She died July 4, 1888.

- Grover L. Bailey was born in Hendricks County, Indiana, December 6, 1889.

- An infant daughter was born in Hendricks County, Indiana, January 31, 1893. Died January

- Clifford Bailey was born in Hendricks County, Indiana, June 15, 1896. Died March 16, 1914.

- Deana W. Bailey was born in Hendricks County, Indiana, April 14, 1898.

- Glen C. Bailey was born in Hendricks County, Indiana, July 8, 1901. Died January 31, 1902.

- Opal C. Bailey was born in Hendricks County, Indiana, May 19, 1903.

<4> **Peter N. Bailey**, [p. 23] second son of John and Rebecca J. Bailey, was born November 26, 1862. He was united in marriage to Clara L. Hall in Hendricks County, Indiana, February 8, 1888. She was born July 21, 1867. Two children were born to this union, viz.:

- William Edgar Bailey, February 12, 1891.

- Martha J. Bailey, born June 1, 1895.

<4> **Susan E. Bailey**, [p. 23] fourth child and third daughter of Rebecca and John Bailey, was united in marriage to Robert T. Hall, December 26, 1888. To this union were born two children, viz.:—

- Marvan Hall, July 18, 1891.

- Bernice M. Hall, May 8, 1901.

<4> **Nettie Bailey**, [p. 23] sixth child of John and Rebecca J. Bailey, his second wife, was born October 11, 1868. She was united in marriage to Ethan A. Leak, February 27, 1887. Ethan A. Leak was born December 18, 1865. Ethan died November 14, 1887. To this union one son was born, viz.:—

- Lyal Leak, April 21, 1888.

Nettie Leak <4> was married the second time, to Harvey Hedge, January 8, 1894. Hedge was born December 2, 1872. To this union were born four children, viz.:—

- Gladys Hedge, August 30, 1896.
- Audry Hedge. November 14, 1900,
- Doris Hedge, November 27, 1902.
- Floyd Hedge, July 30, 1909.

<4> **Nora Bailey**, [p. 23] seventh child of Rebecca and John Bailey, was united in marriage to John W. Lee, July 22, 1894. Five children were born to this union, viz.:—

- Otis Russell Lee, July 4, 1895.
- Jessie Myrtle Lee, June 27, 1897.
- Edith E. Lee, January 12, 1900.
- Rue B. Lee, October 17, 1902.
- Ruby Grace Lee, September 9, 1905.

<4> **Edgar S. Bailey**, [p. 23] eighth child of Rebecca and John Bailey was united in marriage to Lora E. Gibson, February 23, 1898. To this union six children were born, viz.:—

- J. Orvil Bailey, February 17, 1899.
- Gertha M. Bailey, November "6, 1901.
- Clarence E. Bailey, January 8, 1904.
- Infant, born and died October 4, 1909.
- Glen R. Bailey, June 21, 1911.
- Margary M. Bailey, September 14, 1915.

<4> **John T. Bailey**, [p. 23] youngest child of John and Rebecca Bailey was born January 20, 1887, in Hendricks County, Indiana He was united in marriage to Oka May Hudson, Oc-

tober 14 1908. She was born September 30, 1890. One child was born to this union, viz.:—

- Kathleen J. Bailey, October 9, 1914.

Children of Mary Ann (Bailey) McCain <4>
Daughter of Peter and Elizabeth Bailey

<4> **William Solomon McCain**, [p. 23] was united in marriage to Alice Allison, November 13, 1873. Wm. S. McCain's address, St. Paul, Indiana. To this union were born three children, viz.:—

- Charles F. McCain, born August 31, 1874.
- Lulu McCain, born November 24, 1876.
- Wallace McCain, born January 27, 1887.

<4> **Margarette Elizabeth McCain**, [p. 23] second child of Absalom and Mary A. McCain. was united in marriage to John Nash, August 12, 1877. She died October 20, 1890. Four children were born to this union, viz.:—

- Esther Ethel Nash, born May 10, 1881.
- William Nash, born May 9, 1884.
- George W. Nash, born October 12, 1886.
- Emma Frances Nash, born October 1, 1890.

<4> **George Washington McCain**, [p. 23] was united in marriage to Fannie M. West Nov. 11, 1885. Fannie M. West died April 9, 1920. George W. McCain's address is Shelbyville, Indiana. To this union were born four children, viz.—

- Flosie Pearl McCain, born December 24, 1877.
- George Bertram McCain, born January 18, 1880.
- Alonzo Fay McCain, born April 22, 1882.
- Elmer Howard McCain, born July 23, 1887.

<4> **Sabina Jane McCain**, [p. 23] was united in marriage to John Mings, July 1, 1891. Two this union were born two children, viz.:—

- Maud Mings, born July 8, 1892.
- Stacy Mings, born January 24, 1896.

<4> **John Franklin McCain**, [p. 23] was united in marriage to E. Lilly West, August 22, 1878. She died April 26, 1885. To his first marriage were born two children, viz.:—

- Jesse Clarence McCain, born December 2, 1880.
- Cecil Gordon McCain, born February 27, 1885.

John Franklin McCain <4> was married the second time to Amanda Babb, May 30, 1886. To the second marriage were born two children, viz.:—

- Gradie Fern McCain, born July 19, 1890.
- Franklin Paul McCain, born July 3, 1899.

Children of Peter J. Bailey <4>

Son of Peter and Elizabeth Bailey

<4> **Alvin L. Bailey**, [p. 24] was united in marriage to Mary H. Avery, April 8, 1880, in St. Paul, Indiana. Alvin L. Bailey was graduated in medicine by University of Cincinnati, March 4, 1887, with a degree of Master of Arts and Doctor of Medicine. On November 6, 1920, the Honorary Degree of Doctor of Sciences was conferred by the same University. His address is Chesaning, Michigan.

Two children were born to this union, viz.:—

- Clarence W. Bailey, July 23, 1881, died June 30, 1901.
- Ernest Bailey. August 23, 1888, died August 12, 1908.

Alvin L. Bailey <4> was married the second time to Anna May Davidson, June 10, 1890. To this union was born one child, viz.:—

- Lesla Bailey, August 9, 1891, Chesaning, Michigan.

<4> **Daniel V. Bailey**, [p. 24] second child of Phoebe and Peter Bailey united in marriage to Alice L. Stevens in St. Paul, Indiana, January 1, 1884. Daniel died August 9, 1886. One child was born to this union, viz.:—

- Harry Edward Bailey, born May 30, 1885, in St. Paul, Indiana.

<4> **Louis A. Bailey**, [p. 24] was united in marriage to Maud W. Pearson, September 17, 1890. She was born March 26, 1869, in Greensburg, Indiana. To this union one son was born, viz.:—

- Harold Wesley Bailey, born in St. Paul, Indiana, March 3, 1893.

Children of Elizabeth (Bailey) Henderson <4>
Daughter of Peter and Elizabeth Bailey

<4> **Lucinda Henderson**, [p. 24] was united in marriage to Isaac D. Truitt, December 29, 1870. He was born in 1833 and died August 4, 1895.. To this union were born six children, viz.:—

- James B. Truitt, November 11, 1871.
- Walter M. Truitt, December 29, 1872.
- Warren L. Truitt, March 25, 1874.
- Isaac A. Truitt, Jr., November 7, 1876.
- Mary Eva Truitt, September 15, 1879. Died June 3, 1887.
- Ida Alice Truitt, October 22, 1884. Died May 29, 1887.

Lucinda married the second time to John M. Buchanan on February 10, 1897. No children born.

Children of Lidia (Bailey) Roebuck <4>
Daughter of Peter and Elizabeth Bailey

<4> **John H. N. Roebuck**, [p. 24] the sixth child and fourth son of Thomas and Lidia Roebuck was united in marriage to Josephine Smith at Independence, Kansas, August 17, 1891. John H. Roebuck died April 5, 1919. To this union were born twelve children, viz.:—

- Laura Roebuck, January 10, 1893. Died February 14, 1893.
- James W. Roebuck, June 29, 1894. He gave his life for his Country in France, August 8, 1918.
- George Roebuck, (Jr.?), December 10, 1895. Died March 4, 1896.
- John L. Roebuck, December 14, 1896.
- Marie Roebuck, October 19, 1900.
- Jack Roebuck, December 9, 1902. Died July 8, 1908.
- Truman K. Roebuck, March 12, 1905. Died July 14, 1908.
- Lola R. Roebuck, March 24, 1908.
- Louis Roebuck, October 9, 1909.
- Henry Roebuck, March 7, 1912.
- Sarah Roebuck, January, 1914. Died same day.
- Elsie May Roebuck, November 3, 1915. Died same day.

<4> **Emma L. Roebuck**, [p. 24] ninth child and oldest daughter of Lidia and Thomas Roebuck was married to George B. Henson at Colfax, Kansas, October 9, 1890. To this union were born ten children, viz.:—

- Three died in infancy.
- Clarence U. Henson was born August 5, 1891, at Pauhesky, Oklahoma.

- Clyde W. Henson, August 28, 1893, at Coffeeville, Kansas.
- Ethel A Henson, January 23, 1895, at Pauhesky, Oklahoma.
- Ola G. Henson, October 10, 1899, at Claremore, Oklahoma.
- Leona L. Henson, December 26, 1901, at Chautauqua, Kansas.
- Lilly H. Henson, January 15, 1904, at Pauhesky, Oklahoma.
- Charles C. Henson, December 27, 1906, at Silverdale, Kansas.

<4> **Thomas Benton Roebuck**, [p. 24] tenth child of Thomas and Lidia Roebuck was united in marriage to Lou Mosley December 15, 1901, in Sedan, Kansas. There were no children born to this union. They live on a farm near Pahuska, Oklahoma.

<4> **Mary E. Roebuck**, [p. 24] eleventh child and fourth daughter of Thomas and Lidia Roebuck was united in marriage to O. C. Offitt, July 15, 1903, in Sedan, Kansas. To this anion were born six children, viz.:—
- Walter Floyd Offitt, June 2, 1904.
- Olonzo Offitt, (a twin) March 2, 1906, died August 29, 1906.
- Florenzo Offitt, (a twin) March 2, 1906, died September 4, 1906.
- Leo Thomas Offitt, August 8, 1907.
- Frederick George Offitt, March 1, 1911. Died January 19, 1914.
- Oliver Charles Offitt, February 12, 1913. Died June 21, 1913.

To Mary E. Roebuck <4> by a previous marriage, which was not congenial, a divorce followed before this child was born (the mother retained her maiden name), viz.:—
- John Grover Roebuck, February 19, 1896.

<4> **Frances Marion Roebuck**, [p. 24] the twelfth child and ninth son of Lidia and Thomas Roebuck, was united in

marriage to Dessie May Trip, March 3, 1905, in Sedan, Kansas. To this union were born twelve children, viz.:—

- Lilly Emily Roebuck, December 14, 1905.
- Rose Ann Roebuck, May 14, 1907.
- Jennie Pearl Roebuck, June 3, 1908.
- Sadie Marie Roebuck, November 14, 1909
- Seargie Lee Roebuck, March 24, 1911. Died June 27, 1911.
- Lola Irene Roebuck, February 18 1912
- Bessie Ray Roebuck, July 18, 1914.
- Francis Edward Roebuck, January 22, 1916.
- James Ebbon Roebuck, May 20, 1917. Died July 7, 1918.
- Dolly Tawell Roebuck, June 22, 1918.
- Ethel Bell Roebuck, October 25, 1919.
- Johannie Sylvester Roebuck, March 9, 1921.

<4> **Lillie Roebuck**, [p. 24] youngest child of Thomas and Lidia Roebuck married John William Drummond of Elk City, Kansas, November 20, 1904. To this union were born six children, viz.:—

- An infant daughter, December 27, 1905, Elks City, Kansas. Died December 27, 1905
- Thomas Henry Drummond, February 12, 1907, Kanny, Kansas. Died March 18, 1909
- Evalyn Lidia Drummond, June 12, 1910, at Parue, Kansas.
- James Harrison Drummond, March 24, 1913, at Parue, Kansas. Died October 26, 1917.
- William Leonard Drummond, March 29, 1915, at Parue, Kansas. Died October 26, 1917.
- Christine Luella Drummond, May 19, 1917, at Kanny, Kansas. Died October 1, 1918.

Children of Henry Bailey <4>
Son of Peter and Elizabeth Bailey

<4> **Hasson E. Bailey**, [p. 25] was united in marriage to Eva L. Martin, September 21, 1891. No children. Hasson and his splendid wife and helpmate have lived in Douglas, Arizona, where they have engaged in a drug (pharmaceutical) business for some years and have done well.

Children of Absalom Bailey <4>
Son of Peter and Elizabeth Bailey

<4> **Charles C. Bailey**, [p. 25] the oldest living child, was united in marriage to Nancy Elizabeth Lowe, February 4, 1892. She was born November 8, 1873,. and died November 18, 1900. Four children were born to this union, viz.:—

- Dolly May Bailey, born December 5, 1892. Died January 31, 1901.
- Anna Hazel Bailey, born July 9, 1894. Died July 1, 1897.
- Willard Absalom Bailey was born September 26, 1895, and has been a soldier in the U. S. Army for years.
- Dessie Aileen Bailey, born March 21. 1897.

Charles C. Bailey <4> was married the second time to Clara Frances Wilson, June 14, 1901. She was born February 21, 1883. One child was born to this union, viz.:—

- Mildred Lenore Bailey, June 30, 1902.

<4> **Dessie M. Bailey**, [p. 25] was united in marriage to William E. Roberts, August 7, 1893. One child was born, viz.:—

- Cassie E. Roberts, July 4, 1894. Died June 10, 1896.

<4> **James W. Bailey**, [p. 25] was united in marriage to Ida Sophia Louise Stickford, August 16, 1894, Ida was born

November 14, 1874, and died January 7, 1961. Five children were born to this union, viz.:—

- Anna Louise Bailey, January 14, 1898. Died January 8, 1977.
- James Frederick Bailey, October 24, 1900.
- Lucy May Bailey, January 31, 1903. Died February 1, 1974.
- Henry Ebner Bailey, January 29, 1908.
- Irene Gertrude Bailey, September 28, 1910.

<4> **Lola G. Bailey**, [p. 25] was married to D. W. Pearce, August 7, 1899. Two children were born to this union, viz.:—

- Blythe Valentine Pearce, September 17, 1904.
- Wilma Lucille Pearce, May 16, 1907.

GENERATION 5

Children of Elizabeth (3) (Bailey) Britton <5>
Daughter of Nicholas and Sara Ann Bailey

<5> **Sadie E. Britton**, [p. 29] was married to Melvin E. Reser, December 14, 1884. M. E. Reser was born December 12, 1862. Six children were born to this union, viz.:—

- Orvilla Reser was born November 21, 1884.
- Ebert M. Reser, July 21, 1888.
- Blanche E. Reser, November 1, 1890.
- Charles H Reser, December 16, 1893.
- Eveline and Irene Reser (twins) were born August 22, 1895.

  Both died August 29, 1895.

<5> **Mahala Britton**, [p. 29] was married to Charles W. Golding, December 25, 1881. To this union five children were born, viz.:—

- Grace E. Golding, born November 3, 1882.
- George E. Golding, born December 12, 1886
- Esther Q. Golding, born June 20, 1888.
- Estella R. Golding, born July 14, 1904.
- Elizabeth A. Golding, born September 20, 1902.

<5> **Art A. Britton**, [p. 29] was married to Maggie Roberts, February 14, 1902. Maggie Alma Roberts, his wife, born October 28, 1878. (discrepancy in original book – "Married February 14, 1893") Three children were born, viz.:—

- George Britton (2), born January 13, 1895, Marion County, Indiana. Married July 25, 1914.
- Franklin D. Britton, born June 10, 1898, Marion County, Indiana. Married Nov. 3, 1919.
- Ruth J. Britton, born November 15, 1901, Marion County, Indiana. Died February 10, 1903.

48

Children of John P. Bailey <5>

Son of Nicholas and Sarah Ann Bailey

<5> **Heail R. Bailey**, [p. 29] oldest son of John P. and Margaret C. Bailey was married to Helen E. Boland, June 18, 1911. Two children were born to this union, viz.:—

- Jack Edward Bailey, born August 20, 1912.
- Helen M. Bailey September 1, 1918.

<5> **Sarah E. Bailey**, [p. 30] Second child of John P. and Margaret Bailey was married to Charles M. Hamilton. November 18, 1900 five children were born to this union, viz.:—

- Golda M. Hamilton, born July 9, 1902.
- Raymond T. Hamilton, December 4, 1904.
- Delta E. Hamilton, December 13, 1908.
- Wanita E. Hamilton, March 31, 1912.
- Leta Kathryn Hamilton, December 1, 1918.

<5> **Jefferson D. Bailey**, [p. 30] third child of John P. and Margaret Bailey was married to Julia B. Heacock. October 17 1911. One child was born to this union, viz.:—

- Dean Heacock Bailey, born October 29, 1912.

Children of Joseph Wright Bailey <5>

Son of Nicholas and Mary Ellen Bailey

<5> **Golda Alice Bailey**, [p. 30] was married to James Souders, December 25, 1901. She died September 4, 1915. Two children were born to this union viz.:—

- Lucy May Souders, born October 9, 1903.
- Eva May Souders, born April 8, 1905.

<5> **James Oday Bailey**, [p. 30] was married to Lula Brock, June 22, 1913. No children.

<5> **Edith E. Bailey**, [p 30] was married to Fay Henderson, February 22, 1910. One child was born, viz.:—

- Edward F. Henderson, November 24, 1911.

Children of Laura (Bailey) Templeton <5>
Daughter of Nicholas and Mary Ellen Bailey

<5> **Leona M. Templeton**, [p. 30] was united in marriage to Orvil P. Noah, May 29, 1900. Orvil P. Noah was born May 29, 1881. This family resides in Rushville, Rush County, Indiana. To this union were born three daughters, viz.:—

- Fay F. Noah, born December 15, 1901.
- Opal S. Noah, born February 9, 1905.
- Ruthe L. Noah, born February 2, 1911.

Children of Fernando Wood Bailey <5>
Son of Nicholas and Mary Ellen Bailey

<5> **Walter Bailey**, [p. 30] was united in marriage to Flo Mount, August 6, 1907. Walter Bailey died March 11, 1920. To this union two children were born, viz.:—

- Dora Bailey, born June 14, 1908.
- Irene Bailey, born September 30, 1910
-

<5> **Lena G. Bailey**, [p. 30] and Pleasant Dennison were married August 19, 1910. To this union, one son was born, viz.:—

- Richard Bailey Dennison was born July 17, 1914

<5> **Fred Bailey**, [p. 30] and Jennettea Henton were married August 22, 1914. To this union one child was born, viz.:—

- Fernando Francis Bailey born December 9, 1916

<5> **Loyd D. Bailey**, [p. 30] and Berbel Reed were married August 10, 1915. To this union two children were born, viz.:—

- Lyle Bright Bailey, born October 26, 1916.
- Virginia Pauline Bome Bailey, born April 8, 1919.

Children of Nellie (Bailey) Smith <5>
Daughter of Nicholas and Mary Ellen Bailey

<5> **Oral N. Smith**, [p. 31] was married to Edith Doran, May 29, 1912. No children.

<5> **Forest E. Smith**, [p. 31] was married to Maude Ayres, April 2, 1911. No children.

<5> **Mary A. Smith**, [p. 31] was married to Roy Nothern, July 19 1905. To this union were born two children, viz.:—

- William Oliver Nothern, born June 20, 1906.
- Francis Harland Nothern, October 7, 1907.

Children of Van P. Bailey <5>
Son of Nicholas and Mary Ellen Bailey

<5> **Frank P. Bailey**, [p. 31] was united in marriage to Mary Eaglin December, 4, 1912. To this union were born two girls and one boy, viz.:—

- Lydia Bailey born August 12, 1913.
- Sarah Elizabeth Bailey born May 12, 1916.
- Frank William Bailey born October 16, 1918.

<5> **Mary Bailey**, [p. 31] second child and only daughter of Van and Sarah Bailey was united in marriage to Edward Haus,

May 23, 1912. They reside in Wannemaker, IN. To this union was born one boy, viz.:

- Frank Edward Haus, born May 8, 1914.

Children of Warren D. Bailey <5>
Son of Nicholas and Mary Ellen Bailey

<5> **David Bailey**, [p. 31] was married to Margaret Sipe, August 21, 1917. To this union were born two children, viz.:—

- Virginia May Bailey born August 10, 1919.
- Norma Aline Bailey, born February 18, 1922.

Children of James Curtis Bailey <5>
Son of Nicholas and Mary Ellen Bailey

<5> **George (2) Bailey**, [p. 32] was married to Frances M. Walker May 9, 1919. To this union was born one child, viz.:—

- Curtis LeRoy Bailey, October 10, 1920.

<5> **Grace Bailey**, [p. 32] was married to Paul Estborn, February 15, 1921. To this union was born one child, viz.:—

- Dortha Jane Estborn, March 15, 1922.

Children of William A. Pearce <5>
Son of Rossell and Susan Pearce

<5> **Estelle F. Pearce**, [p. 32] oldest child of William Pearce, was married to William Atikson, March 18, 1888, in Finney County, Kansas. Two children were born to this union, viz.:—

- Earnest Tyler Atikson, born February 2, 1889, in Hodgeman County, Kansas.
- Jennie Atikson, born March 21, 1896, in Oklahoma .

<5> **Claud F. Pearce**, [p. 32] second child of William Pearce was united in marriage to Ora A. Hart, January 18, 1892, at Ravana, Kansas. Six children were born to this union, viz.:—

- Zella M. Pearce, born January 29, 1893.
- Zulla F. Pearce, born October 30, 1894.
- Paul F. Pearce, born July 23, 1896.
- Claud A. Pearce, born March 6, 1898. He died July 20, 1899.
- Leora E. Pearce, born July 16, 1899.
- Tiny Blossom Pearce, born February 5, 1901. Died February 5, 1901.

<5> **Charles D. Pearce**, [p. 32] second son of William Pearce was born in Hendricks County, and united in marriage to Eva Jane Coen, August 28, 1901. No children born.

<5> **Mary J. Pearce**, [p. 32] second daughter and fourth child of William A. and Elizabeth Pearce, was united in marriage to E. W. Killon, February 27, 1898, at Emmins, Kansas. Mr. Killon is a minister of the gospel of the Church of Christ. Two sons were born to this union, viz.:—

- Infant, a son, born on December 17, 1898 and died four days later.
- Lyle L. Killon was born July 27, 1910, at Canton, Mo.

<5> **Cecil V. Pearce**, [p. 32] fifth child of William A. and Elizabeth Pearce was married to Ella N. Ellern, February 1, 1904, at Garden City, Kansas. Mr. Pearce is a minister of the Gospel, as is also his wife of the Church of Christ. No children.

<5> **Nellie D. Pearce**, [p. 32] youngest daughter of William A. and Elizabeth Pearce was united in marriage to Floyd B. Taylor at Canton, Mo., June 15, 1909. To this union one child was born, viz.:—

- Infant, a son, February 27, 1911. He died in a couple of days.

Children of Mary Edna (Pearce) Woodard <5>
Daughter of Rossell and Susan Pearce

<5> **Viola May Woodard**, [p. 32] was married to Ara C. Caldwell, April 23, 1885, in Boone County, Indiana.

<5> **Raymond Thurman Woodard**, [p. 33] was united in marriage to Elfie Anderson, January 2, 1908, in Atchison, Kansas.

<5> **Nelly Ester Woodard**, [p. 33] the third child of Mary Edna and William Woodard was united in marriage to George E Adler on July 5, 1891, in Kansas. Their address is Horton, Kansas. Six children were born to this union, viz.:—

- George Alberts Adler, born April 30, 1893, in Kansas.
- Nellie May Adler, born September 2, 1894, in Nebraska
- Ethel Delphine Adler, born November 18, 1896, in Nebraska.
- Raymond LeRoy Adler, born July 12, 1899, in Nebraska.
- Clarence Earnest Adler, born April 16, 1901, in Nebraska.
- Frayne Chilton Adler, born April 13, 1904, in Nebraska.

<5> **Irving Clyde Woodard**, [p. 33] was married to Ivy Mc-Donald, July 16 1899, in Kansas. To this union were born three children, viz.:—

- Mona Andry Woodard was born March 31, 1900.
- Lanford Donald Woodard was born October 12, 1906.
- Willa Wyvitte Woodard, February 18, 1913.

Children of Charles M. Pearce <5>
Son of Rossell and Susan Pearce

<5> **Tessie Maud Pearce**, [p. 33] was married to John Pebble, June 25, 1900. To this union were born two children,

viz.:—

- Eva M. Pebble, born May 1, 1902, in Richardson County, Nebraska.
- Daisy Iowa Pebble, born, September 12, 1904 in Pottamatomie County, Iowa.

<5> William Leslie Pearce, [p. 33] was married to Pauline Harrison December 7, 1912. To this union were born two children, viz.:—

- Burnell Leslie Pearce was born June 16, 1915, in Richardson County, Nebraska.
- Genevia Adaline Pearce was born November 26, 1917, in Richardson County, Nebraska.

Children of George Thomas Pearce <5>

Son of Rossell and Susan Pearce

<5> Arie Beaughn Pearce, [p. 33] was married to Arthur Whitzel, January 21, 1903 in Sterling, Kansas. To this marriage was born, viz.:—

- Paul Pearce Whitzel, October 20, 1903.

Arie Beaughn <5> was divorced from Whitzel March 18, 1904, and was married to J. J. Hazlett, November 29, 1909. They reside in Sterling, Kansas. To this union was born, viz.:—

- Harold Dale Hazlett, July 23, 1911.

<5> Vera May Pearce, [p. 33] was united in marriage to Bert G. Woodard of Hutchinson, Kansas, on October 30, 1906. They still reside there.

<5> Vella Maude Pearce, [p. 33] was married to Robert E. Wyatt, November 19, 1910, at Sterling, Kansas. Vella Maude died of birth complications. To this union was born, viz.:—

- Robert E. Wyatt, Jr., July 3, 1920.

<5> **Amy Leona Pearce**, [p. 33] was married to Cecil C. Hazlett, September 12, 1919. They live in Sterling, Kansas.

Children of Eva Ann (Bailey) Campbell <5>
Daughter of John and Catherine Bailey

<5> **Mary C. Campbell**, [p. 34] united in marriage to Tilman Bush, March 10, 1895. One child was born to this union, viz.:—

- Louis A. Bush in Clay County, Indiana, January 9, 1896.

<5> **John L. Campbell**, [p. 34] united in marriage to Ethel Brown, June 7, 1903. To this union six children were born, viz.:—

- Infant, no information.
- Edith G. Campbell, born in Vigo County, Indiana, May 30, 1905.
- Eva Alma Campbell, born in Vigo County, Indiana, April 22, 1907.
- Frances B. Campbell, born in Vigo County, Indiana, July 23, 1909.
- Kenneth B. Campbell, born in Vigo County, Indiana, July 3, 1911.
- Delbert E. Campbell, born in Vigo County, Indiana, December 30, 1918.

<5> **Martin O. Campbell**, [p. 34] was united in marriage to Blanche Brown in 1904. To this union two children were born, viz.:—

- Juanita L. Campbell was born in Sullivan County, Indiana, February 25, 1905.
- Trilby M. Campbell was born in Sullivan County, Indiana, November 8, 1907.

<5> **Oliver D. Campbell**, [p. 34] was united in marriage to Pearl Grimmes in 1905. To this union four children were born, viz.:—

- Everett W. Campbell, born in Sullivan County, Indiana, November 30, 1905.

- Harold E. Campbell, (twin) born in Sullivan County, Indiana, July 13, 1908.

- Gearld E. Campbell, (twin) born in Sullivan County, Indiana, July 13, 1908. Died July 13, 1908.

- Geneva V. Campbell, born in Sullivan County, Indiana, April 23, 1911, died December 8, 1912.

<5> **Sarah E. Campbell**, [p. 34] united in marriage to Emmett E. Power August 28, 1910. To this union three children were born, viz.:—

- Helen M. Power, born in Sullivan County, Indiana, June 8, 1911.

- Vernal E. Power, born in Sullivan County, Indiana, January 4, 1913.

- Victor E. Power, born in Vigo County, Indiana, October 18, 1914.

<5> **Eva A. Campbell**, [p. 34] daughter of Martin and Eva Ann, was united in marriage to Phillip Pratt, February 7, 1915.. To this union two children were born, viz.:—

- William M. Pratt, Marion County, Indiana, October 2, 1916.

- Carl R. Pratt, Marion County, Indiana, August 31, 1919.

<5> **James M Campbell**, [p. 34] united in marriage to Lois A. Copeland, August 16, 1916. To this union three children were born, viz.:—

- Oris M. Campbell, in Vigo County, Indiana, March 23, 1917.

- Elvin E. Campbell, in Vigo County, Indiana, February 22, 1919.

- Ruth G. Campbell, in Vigo County, Indiana, February 5, 1920.

Children of Marion Bailey <5>

Son of John and Catherine Bailey

<5> **Harry E. Bailey**, [p. 35] married to Dora M. Brown, December 16, 1903. She was born January 11, 1883, in Vigo County, Indiana. Two children were born to this union, viz.:—

- Buford E. Bailey, June 2, 1906, in Hendricks County, Indiana.
- Vileta D. Bailey, November 13, 1908, in Hendricks County, Indiana.

<5> **Artie M. Bailey**, [p. 35] second son of Marion Bailey was married to Nora E. Coombs, October 6, 1906. She was born September 4, 1886, in Boone County, Indiana. To this union were born four children, viz.:—

- Kenneth R. Bailey, January 2, 1908, Boone County, Indiana.
- Earl E. Bailey, December 20, 1911, Boone County, Indiana
- Ruby G. Bailey. June 24, 1914, Boone County, Indiana.
- Viora Caroline Bailey, July 2, 1918, Boone County, Indiana.

<5> **Luna A. Bailey**, [p. 35] only daughter of Marion and Rachel C. Bailey was united in marriage to Andrew S. Pritchett, August 6, 1905. He was born August 8, 1881, in Hendricks County, Indiana. To this union were born four children, viz.:—

- Ruby T. Pritchett, born May 29, 1909, Hendricks County, Indiana.
- Lowell E. Pritchett, December 31, 1911, Hendricks County, Indiana.
- Jewell B. Pritchett, October 27, 1914, Boone County, Indiana.
- Charles E. Pritchett, June 11, 1916, Hendricks County, Indiana.

<5> **Goldie V. Bailey**, [p. 35] third son of Marion and Rachel Bailey was united in marriage to Ruth Ann Keeney, November 9, 1912. She was born in Hendricks County, Indiana, September , 1891. To this union were born two children, viz.:—

- Ronold Marion Bailey, January 2, 1914, Hendricks County,
- Richard Wayne Bailey, December 2, 1917, Hendricks County, Indiana.

Children of Mary M. (Bailey) Dale <5>

Daughter of John and Rebecca Bailey, his second wife.

<5> **Ira O. Dale**, [p. 35] was united in marriage to Sarah E. Leak, January 9, 1886. To this union one child was born, viz.:—

- Susie Fern Dale, born May 12, 1909.

<5> **W. Edgar Dale**, [p. 35] was united in marriage to Donnie Tramwell, February 4, 1902. To this union were born one child, viz.:—

- William C. Dale, born August 16, 1911.

<5> **Charles B. Dale**, [p. 35] was united in marriage to Della Eggers, August 21, 1904. To this union two children were born, viz.:—

- Herbert S. Dale, August 7, 1906.
- Marian June Dale, June 17, 1916.

Children of George W. Bailey <5>

Son of John and Rebecca Bailey, his second wife.

<5> **Fannie J. Bailey**, [p. 35] oldest child of George W. Bailey was married to Alva Hocker, March 12, 1913. One child was born to this union:

- Keith B. Hocker, June 5, 1918, in Hendricks County, Indiana.

<5> **Grover L. Bailey**, [p. 35] third child of George W. and Hattie Bailey, was married to Vaughn Duncan, April 14, 1915. No children.

<5> **Deana W. Bailey**, [p. 36] sixth child of George W. and Hattie Bailey was married to Orvil Wills, February 21, 1918. Two children were born to this union, viz.:—

- Lavina A. Wills, January 21, 1919.
- Nellie B. Wills, August 12, 1920.

Children of Peter N. Bailey <5>

Son of John and Rebecca Bailey, his second wife.

<5> **William Edgar Bailey**, [p. 36] was united in marriage to Vida E. Ragsdale, February 29, 1912. She was born October 4, 1890.

Children of Susan E. (Bailey) Hall <5>

Daughter of John and Rebecca Bailey, his second wife.

<5> **Marvan Hall**, [p. 36] oldest child of Susan E. Bailey and Robert Hall, was united in marriage to Clara Scott, June, 1918. No children.

<5> **Bernice Hall**, [p. 36] second child of Susan E. and Robert Hall, was married to Robert Ratcliff, August 28, 1920. One child was born September 8, 1920, viz.:—

- Oral Hall Ratcliff.

Children of Nettie (Bailey) Leak <5>

Daughter of John and Rebecca Bailey, his second wife.

<5> **Lyal Leak**, [p. 36] son of Ethan and Nettie Leak, was married to Edith Rose, December 29, 1917. To this union two sons were born, viz.:—

- John Mac Leak, May 28, 1920.
- Richard L. Leak, born April 28, 1922.

Children of Nettie (Bailey) Hedge <5>

<5> **Gladys Hedge**, [p. 37] was united in marriage to George L. Salb, January 15, 1914. Salb was born April 3, 1886. There were born to this union five children, viz.:—

- One son still born April 15, 1916.
- Maxine T. Salb, February 14, 1917.
- Madeline G. Salb, September 3, 1918. She died November 22, 1918.
- Margaret M. Salb, September 2, 1920.
- Bettie J. Salb, June 2, 1922.

Children of Nora (Bailey) Lee <5>

Daughter of John and Rebecca Bailey, his second wife.

<5> **Otis Russell Lee**, [p. 37] was married to Minnie Hamlock, February 17, 1921. To this union one child was born, viz.:—

- Lewana Lee, August 8, 1921.

<5> **Jessie Myrtle Lee**, [p. 37] was married to Clinton B. Miller, February 11, 1916. To this union one child was born, viz.:—

- Jessie Lawrence Miller, January 20, 1917. She died January 27, 1917.

<5> **Edith E. Lee**, [p. 37] was married to Roy E. Sinks, November 16, 1920. To this union was born one son, viz.:—

- John LeRoy Sinks, October 6, 1921.

Children of Edgar S. Bailey <5>

Son of John and Rebecca Bailey, his second wife.

<5> **J. Orvil Bailey**, [p. 37] was married to Elsie L. Randal, December 19, 1917. To this union was born one child, viz.:—

- Clyde Ugene Bailey, born July 22, 1921.

<5> **Gertha M. Bailey**, [p. 37] was married to Estle D. Ray, October 26, 1921.

Children of William Solomon McCain <5>
Son of Absalom and Mary Ann McCain

<5> **Charles F. McCain**, [p. 38] oldest child of William S. and Alice McCain was married to Margaret Philips, February 14, 1898. Five children were born to this union, viz.:—

- Eva McCain, born May 8, 1900. Died August 11, 1900.
- Grady Ruth McCain, born August 15, 1902.
- John W. McCain, born December 80, 1904.
- Rena McCain, born June 19, 1908.
- Alice R.. McCain, born October 21, 1916.

<5> **Lulu McCain**, [p. 38] second child of William S. and Alice McCain was united in marriage to Robert Parker, February 24, 1900. Three children were born to this union, viz.:—

- Maurice Parker, born December 23, 1902.
- Jessie M. Parker, born October 18, 1904.
- Alice L. Parker, born April 7, 1909.

<5> **Wallace McCain**, [p. 38] second son of William S. and Alice McCain, was united in marriage to Grace Riser, July 6, 1907. His address is St. Paul, Indiana. To this union were born two children, viz.:—

- William Frederick McCain, born February 28, 1909.
- Mary Alice McCain, born October 29, 1912.

Children of Margarette Elizabeth (McCain) Nash <5>
Daughter of Absalom and Mary Ann McCain

<5> **Esther Ethel Nash**, [p. 38] was united in marriage to Clyde Lingenfelter, March 7, 1903. No children.

<5> **William Nash**, [p. 38] oldest son of John and Margaret E. Nash, was united in marriage to Cecil Hogan, March 9, 1904. To this union was born one son, viz.:—

- Walter Clyde Nash, born July 8, 1906.

William Nash <5> was married a second time to Lilly (?), October 13, 1911. To this union were born four children, viz.:—

- George William Nash, born March 6, 1913.
- Alfred LeRoy Nash, born August 6, 1915.
- Scott Ray Nash, born April 6, 1918.
- Lucinda May Nash, born January 15, 1920.

<6> **George W. Nash**, [p. 38] son of John and Margarette Nash was married, no children.

<5> **Emma Frances Nash**, [p. 38] was united in marriage to Alfred Estell, September 4, 1913. To this union was born one child, viz.:—

- Virginia M. Estell, born April 2, 1922.

Children of George W. McCain <5>
Son of Absalom and Mary Ann McCain

<5> **Flosie Pearl McCain**, [p. 38] was united in marriage to James R. Howe, December 24, 1899. To this union were born two children, viz.: —

- Lola Marie Howe, born April 23, 1908.
- Beatrice Arletta Howe, born May 4, 1911.

<5> **George Bertram McCain**, [p. 38] oldest son of George W. and Fannie McCain, was united in marriage to Lilly Mirtle Gray, February 26, 1903. No children.

<5> **Alonzo Fay McCain**, [p. 38] second son of Geo. W. and Fannie McCain, was united in marriage to Alice Carrie Bruner, September 30, 1906. To this union were born five children, viz.:—

- George Raymond McCain, born November 28, 1907.
- Charles Herbert McCain, born January 18, 1910.
- Edith Faye McCain, born June 12, 1912.
- Ruth Maxine McCain, born March 19, 1914.
- Marjorie Lucile McCain, born December 27, 1915.

<5> **Elmer Howard McCain**, [p. 38] third son of George W. and Fannie McCain, was united in marriage to Ida Elizabeth Drager, February 18, 1913. No children.

Children of Sabina Jane (McCain) Mings <5>
Daughter of Absalom and Mary Ann McCain

<5> **Maud Mings**, [p. 39] was united in marriage to Harry C. Brown, December 18, 1912. He died September 2, 1918. No children.

<5> **Stacy Mings**, [p. 39] was united in marriage to Ernest C. Collier, October 2, 1914. To this union were born two children, viz.:—

- John W. Collier, born September 6, 1916.
- Elizabeth Collier, born August 7, 1909.

Children of John Franklin McCain <5>

Son of Absalom and Mary Ann McCain

<5> **Jesse Clarence McCain**, [p. 39] was united in marriage to Maude M. Cherry, October 29, 1902. To this union were born two children, viz.:—

* Aletha Cherry McCain, born July 28, 1904.
* Justine Frances McCain, born July 30, 1911.

<5> **Cecil Gordon McCain**, [p. 39] was united in marriage to Martha L. Wahl, October 16, 1907. No children.

Children of John Franklin and Amanda McCain, his second wife.

<5> **Gradie Fern McCain**, [p. 21] was united in marriage to Claud Cherry, February 25, 1909. Died December 27, 1918. One child was born to this union, viz.:—

* Rita Fern Cherry, born October 12, 1910.

<5> **Franklin Paul McCain**, [p. 39] was united in marriage to Treca Conner, September 14, 1919. To this union two children were born, viz.:—

* Wanetta Fern McCain, born August 12, 1921.
* Merrill M. McCain, born August 26, 1922, in Shelby County, Indiana.

Generation Children of Alvin L. Bailey <5>

Son of Peter J. and Phoebe Bailey

<5> **Lesla Bailey**, [p. 40] was united in marriage to Edward Miller of Chesaning, Michigan, November 24, 1913. To this union three children have been born, viz.:—

* Bob Miller, October 12, 1914.
* Edson Miller, January 11, 1916.
* Maryland Miller, August 7, 1919.

Children of Daniel V. Bailey <5>

Son of Peter J. and Phoebe Bailey

<5> **Harry Edward Bailey**, [p. 40] was united in marriage to Beatrice R. McHugh, November 21, 1906. She was born December 3, 1887. To this union were born seven children, viz.—

- Norval Bailey, born January 20, 1908. Died January 21, 1908.
- DeLoris Bailey, born January, 1909.
- Burnelle Bailey, born October 14, 1913
- Daniel V. Bailey, born January 6. 1916.
- Harry E. Bailey (2), born March 19, 1917.
- Joan J. Bailey, born April, 1918.
- Esther E. Bailey, born January 3, 1921.

Children of Louis A. Bailey <5>

Son of Peter J. and Phoebe Bailey

<5> **Harold Wesley Bailey**, [p. 40] was united in marriage in Los Angeles, California, to Clara Doeset June 30, 1913. They reside at 120 West 68th Place, Los Angeles, California.

Children of Lucinda (Henderson) Truitt <5>

Daughter of Joseph and Elizabeth Henderson

<5> **James B. Truitt**, [p. 40] oldest child of Isaac and Lucinda Henderson Truitt, was married to Leola Holland, March 20, 1913. To this union was born one daughter, viz.:—

- Nadine Alice Truitt, born June 4, 1915.

<5> **Walter M. Truitt**, [p. 40] second child of Isaac and Lucinda Henderson Truitt, was united in marriage in Cripple Creek, Colorado, August 6. 1901, (wife ?). Two children were born to this union, viz.:—

- Ora Alice Truitt, Denver, Colorado, May 11, 1902. She died in Los Angeles, California, April 30, 1919.

- Ada Frances Truitt, born in Cripple Creek, California, April 27, 1903. His address is Limbershine, California.

<5> **Warren L. Truitt**, [p. 40] third son of Isaac and Lucinda Truitt, was married in Denver, Colorado, May 20, 1896, to Elizabeth Omard. To this union four children were born, viz.:—

- James Francis Truitt, Denver, Colorado, May 11, 1897. He died in Elston, Colorado, October 1, 1911.
- Edward Truitt, Denver, Colorado, July 2, 1900. He died in Denver, Colorado, January 7, 1904.
- Warren Lee Truitt, Denver, Colorado, September 13, 1904.
- Margaret Elizabeth Truitt, Gold Field, Colorado, July 27, 1908. His address is Vantura, California.

Children of John H. N. Roebuck <5>
Son of Thomas and Lidia Roebuck

<5> **James W. Roebuck**, [p. 41] oldest son of John and Josephine Roebuck, arrived at manhood, was married to Eva Mames, June 28, 1913.

<5> **John L. Roebuck**, [p. 41] was united in marriage to Maggie Hendricks, July 5, 1921.

<5> **Marie Roebuck**, [p. 41] was united in marriage to Grover McKenzie. One child was born to this union, viz.:—

- Edna McKenzie, born July 19, 1922.

Children of Emma (Roebuck) Henson <5>
Daughter of Thomas and Lidia Roebuck

<5> **Clarence U. Henson**, [p. 41] oldest child of Emma and George Henson, was united in marriage to Zola Waldon, May 22, 1913. To this union were born two children, viz.:—

- Edna Alberta Henson, July 27, 1914.
- Jennie F. Henson, May 29, 1916.

Children of Mary E. (Roebuck) Offitt <5>
Daughter of Thomas and Lidia Roebuck

<5> **John Grover Roebuck**, [p. 42] (his mother retained her maiden name after a previous brief marriage) was united in marriage to Sarah Baun, June 21, 1918, in Arkansas City, Kansas. No children were born.

Children of Charles C. Bailey <5>
Son of Absalom and Elizabeth Bailey

<5> **Dessie Aileen Bailey**, [p. 44] was united in marriage to Clifford Bogerman, July 30, 1914. Two children were born to this union, viz.:—

* Ruth Elizabeth Bogerman, October 1, 1915.
* Charles Clifford Bogerman, March 30, 1919.

Children of James W. Bailey <5>
Son of Absalom and Elizabeth Bailey

<5> **Anna Louise Bailey**, [p. 44] was united in marriage on November 27, 1935 to Neal Oliver Diener in St. Paul, Indiana. She died January 8, 1977. To this union two children were born, viz.:—

* Ella Marie Diener, November 28, 1936.
* Albert Neal Diener, January 15, 1943.

<5> **James Frederick Bailey**, [p. 44] was married to Leona Pearl Jones, August 27, 1919. Leona Pearl died on February 28, 1929. He died April, 1997. To this union were born three children, viz.:—

* Ida Louise Bailey, (a twin) May 5, 1921.
* Bertha Lucille Bailey, (a twin) May 5, 1921.
* William Frederick Bailey, March 25, 1925.

James Frederick Bailey <5> married a second time to Margaret (Hicks) Worland on May 30, 1930. Margaret died January 19, 1979 in Indianapolis, Indiana. To this marriage were born four children, viz.:—

- Joan Bailey, born July 19, 1931 in Shelby County, Indiana.
- Shirley Sue Bailey, born July 1935, died September 1935 in Shelby County, Indiana.
- Mary Margaret Bailey, (a twin) born May 26, 1940 in Shelby County, Indiana.
- James Robert Bailey, (a twin) born May 26, 1940 in Shelby County, Indiana.

James Frederick Bailey <5> was married a third time to Mary (Isham) Mertz in July 1979 in Indianapolis, Indiana. Mary was born January 21, 1908. No children.

<5> **Lucy May Bailey**, [p. 45] was married to Delbert Kerr, December 27, 1919. Delbert Farlow Kerr was born April 16, 1900. She died February 1, 1974. Two children were born to this union, viz.:—

- James Delbert Kerr, born May 25, 1924
- Mary Jean Kerr, born April 28, 1926.

<5> **Henry Ebner Bailey**, [p. 45] was united in marriage to Lois MacAbery on August 12, 1944. He died January 25, 1985, and his wife died in 1982. To this union two children were born, viz.:—

- Earl Ebner Bailey, born December 30, 1945.
- Ruth Irene Bailey, born May 21, 1948.

<5> **Irene G. Bailey**, [p. 45] was united in marriage to William Henry Chellberg on September 27, 1930 at St. Paul, Indiana. William died January 24, 1988, and she died Decem-

ber 22, 2000. To this union four children were born, viz.:—

- William Sidney Chellberg, born September 14, 1936.
- Donna Sue Chellberg, born July 25, 1938.
- Thomas Ebner Chellberg, born January 9, 1941.
- Lois Irene Chellberg, born January 6, 1944.

GENERATION 6

Children of Sadie E. Reser (Britton) <6>

Daughter of George and Elizabeth Britton

<6> **Orvilla Reser**, [p. 48] was married to John Booth, May 12, 1919. To this union was born one child, viz.:—

- John Booth, Jr., August 15, 1922.

<6> **Ebert M. Reser**, [p. 48] was married to Bernice Miller, March 16, 1912. One child was born, viz.:—

- Lawrence Reser, January 4, 1913.

<6> **Charles H. Reser**, [p.48] was married to Margaret Loutzl, August 22, 1920. No children.

Children of Mahala Golding (Britton) <6>

Daughter of George and Elizabeth Britton

<6> **Grace E. Golding**, [p. 48] as was married to John T. Summers, October l, 1901. Four children were born to this union, viz.: —

- Ruth Summers, born August 27, 1902.
- John V. Summers, born October 12, 1907.
- Ermatine J. Summers, born October 19, 1909.
- Eda Merl Summers, born July 1, 1913.
-

<6> **George E. Golding**, [p. 48] was married to Irine Collens, May 8, 1908. To this union were born two children, viz.: —

- Charles W. Golding (2), January 23 1908.
- Mildred J. Golding, November 19, 1909.

<6> **Esther Q. Golding**, [p. 48] was married to Frank E. Grote, March 21, 1906. Three children were born to this union, viz.: —

- Laurence Grote, born May 19, 1908. Died in 8 days.
- Donald A. Grote, August 10, 1910.
- Margaret E. Grote, April 27, 1911.

<6> **Elizabeth A. Golding**, [p. 48] was married to Edward L. Wilkert, August 16, 1913. No children.

<6> **Estella R. Golding**, [p. 48] was married to Homer Clark, November 6, 1915. No children.

Children of Sarah E. Hamilton (Bailey) <6>
Daughter of John P. and Margaret Bailey

<6> **Golda M. Hamilton**, [p. 49] oldest child of Sarah E. and Charles Hamilton was married to Halsey Reeves, September 22, 1919

Children of Estelle F. (Pearce) Atikson <6>
Daughter of William A. and Elizabeth Pearce

<6> **Ernest T. Atikson**, [p. 52] oldest son of Estelle F. Pearce was married to Edith Bell Dobson, October 26, 1910, in Cherokee, Okla. Six Children were born to this union, viz.: —

- Rena Orline Atikson, May 2, 1911, born in Fargo, Oklahoma
- Katherine May Atikson, March 22, 1913, born in Fargo, Oklahoma
- Loren Russell Atikson, July 1, 1914, born in Fargo, Oklahoma
- Gilma Juel Atikson, July 28, 1915, born in Fargo, Oklahoma
- Alma Lucille Atikson, December 10, 1916, born in Fargo, Oklahoma
- Roland Ernest Atikson, February 23, 1920, born in Fargo, Oklahoma.

<6> **Jennie Atikson**, [P. 32] daughter of Estelle Pearce married Henry Jakay, October 16, 1913. Four children were born to this union. viz.: —

- Samuel W. Jakay, born August 18, 1914, born in Fargo, Oklahoma.
- Pauline W. Jakay, born January 27, 1916, born in Fargo, Oklahoma.
- Hoener T. Jakay, February 26, 1918, born in Fargo, Oklahoma.
- Sidney A. Jakay, was born December 20, 1919, born in Fargo, Oklahoma.

Children of Claud F. Pearce <6>
Son of William A. and Elizabeth Pearce

<6> **Zella M. Pearce**, [p. 53] was married to Theron P. Smith at Port Arthur, Texas, October 31, 1914. Adopted a little girl three years old by the name of Coralie Helen Pearce, in 1918.

<6> **Zulla F. Pearce**, [p. 53] married George M. Center of Port Arthur, Texas, October 31, 1912. To this union one child was born, Zulla Pearce Center died January 8, 1915, in Kansas.

- George Center, Jr., July 6, 1914, who only lived four days, dying July 10.

Children of Louis A. Bush <6>
Son of Tilman and Mary C. Bush

[Ed. Note: We believe that Louis A. and Ardie L. are the same person.]

<6> **Ardrie L. Bush**, [p. 56] (One grandson of Eva Bailey Campbell.) was united in marriage to Grace Freeland in 1915. To this union two children were born, viz.: —

- Tilman W. Bush, born in Marion County, Indiana, September 17, 1917.
- Paul A. Bush, born in Marion County, Indiana, September 28, 1920.

Children of Anna Louise (Bailey) Diener <6>
Daughter of James W. and Ida Bailey

<6> **Ella Marie Diener**, [p. 68] was united in marriage to John Owens in DuPage County, Illinois on August 17, 1968. To this union was born, viz.: —

- Lori Ann Owens, born February 24, 1971.

<6> **Albert Neal Diener**, [p. 68] was united in marriage to Karen May Chellberg in Wheaton, DuPage County, IL in May 1963. To this union were born, viz.: —

- Sarah Marie Diener
- Sharon Diener
- James Albert Diener
- Judith Ann Diener
- Diane Diener born August, 1978.
- Roy Diener born June 1982.
- Michael Diener born January, 1984.

Children of James Frederick Bailey <6>
Son of James W. and Ida Bailey

<6> **Ida Louise Bailey,** [p. 68] was united in marriage to Alfred Hogan in Decatur County, Indiana on February 8, 1941. To this union were born, viz.: —

- Stephen E. Hogan, born May 25, 1942 in Shelby County, Indiana.
- Alfred Anthony Hogan, born March 18, 1946 in Shelby County, Indiana.
- Daniel Lee Hogan, born February 12, 1949 in Shelby County, Indiana.

Ida Louise Bailey <6> was married again to John Keith Humfleet in July, 1955, and divorced July 2, 1959. No children.

<6> **Bertha Lucille Bailey**, [p. 49] was united in marriage to LaVern Schuberth on August 28, 1952 at Wheaton, DuPage County, IL. Divorced in 1985. To this union were born, viz.: —

- James Timothy Schuberth, born April 7, 1957 at Council Bluffs, Ia. Died November, 2000 in Omaha, NE.
- Thomas Frederick Schuberth, born May 15, 1961 Council Bluffs, Ia.

<6> **William Frederick Bailey**, [p. 68] was united in marriage to Esther Dale on June 3, 1945 in Shelby County, Indiana. William died November 11, 1973. To this union were born, viz.: —

- Leona Pearl Bailey, born March 12, 1946 at Los Angeles, California.
- Cynthia Bailey, born June 14, 1953 at Los Angeles, California.

<6> **Joan Bailey**, [p. 69] was united in marriage to Carl Lucas, Jr. On August 2, 1951. To this union were born, viz.:—

- Gary Phillip Lucas, born August 21, 1953 in Shelby County, Indiana.
- Dawn Janine Lucas, born August 29, 1955 in Shelby County, Indiana.

<6> **Mary Margaret Bailey**, [p. 69] was united in marriage to David Barber in Indianapolis, Indiana on September 23, 1961. To this were born, viz.:—

- Allen Lee Barber, born July 27, 1969 at Marshall, Minnesota.
- Brian David Barber, born July 15, 1972 at Marshall, Minnesota.

<6> **James Robert Bailey**, [p. 69] was united in marriage to Marjorie Robertson on March 4, 1960. To this union were born, viz.: —

- Derrick Edward Bailey, born January 3, 1961 in Marion County, Indiana, died January 7, 1961.

- Darren James Bailey, born May 5, 1962 in Marion County, Indiana.
- Denise Elaine Bailey, born September 20, 1963 in Marion County, Indiana.
- Danine Joan Bailey, born March 27, 1965 in Marion County, Indiana.
- Lynette Michelle Bailey, born November 12, 1966 in Marion County, Indiana.
- James Carl Bailey, born October 2, 1969 in Marion County, Indiana.

Children of Lucy May (Bailey) Kerr <6>
Daughter of James W. and Ida Bailey

<6> **James Delbert Kerr**, [p. 69] was united in marriage to Norma Lou Pickett on September 26, 1944. He died March 12, 2013 and is buried in Lewis Creek Baptist Cemeatary. To this union were born, viz.: —

- Vicky Lynn Kerr, born June 11, 1948 in Shelby County, Indiana.
- James Michael Kerr, born June 29, 1958 in Shelby County, Indiana.
- Byron Dean Kerr, born November 19, 1965 in Shelby County, Indiana. Died September 22, 1985.

<6> **Mary Jean Kerr**, [p. 69] was united in marriage to John Milton Thomas on December 24, 1946. To this union were born, viz.: —

- Marsha Thomas, born September, 1947.
- Mark Thomas
- Melinda Thomas
- Melanie Thomas

Children of Henry Ebner Bailey <6>
Son of James W. and Ida Bailey

<6> **Earl Ebner Bailey**, [p. 69] was united in marriage to Ruth Ann Brown on November 13, 1965 in Cleveland, Ohio.

To this union were born, viz.: —

- Beverly Ruth Bailey, born November 8, 1966.
- Daniel Ebner Bailey, born September 2, 1969.
- Sandra Ann Bailey, born August 28, 1970.

<6> **Ruth Irene Bailey**, [p. 69] received her M.D. degree from Indiana University on May 13, 1979. She opened an office of Internal Medicine in Lapel, Indiana on June 1, 1982. She ceased medical practice in about 1986 and became an author.

Children of Irene G. (Bailey) Chellberg <6>
Daughter of James W. and Ida Bailey

<6> **William Sidney Chellberg**, [p. 70] was united in marriage to Doris Jean Paskewitz on June 20, 1956 at Lucan, Redwood County, Minnesota. To this union were born, viz.: —

- Kevin John Chellberg, born May 1, 1957 in Geneva, Illinois.
- Cheryl Lynn Chellberg, born April 29, 1960 in St. Charles, Illinois.
- Gary Merlin Chellberg, born September 8, 1962 in St. Charles, Illinois.

<6> **Donna Sue Chellberg**, [p. 70] was united in marriage to Lloyd Paskewitz on May 7, 1959 at Wheaton, DuPage County, Illinois. To this union were born, viz.: —

- Ronald Dean Paskewitz, born July 16, 1960
- Sandra Kay Paskewitz
- Beverly Sue Paskewitz
- Rebecca Jill Paskewitz, born April 16, 1968
- Lori Ann Paskewitz, born October, 1975.
- Tim Paskewitz, born December 1977.

<6> **Thomas Ebner Chellberg**, [p. 70] was united in marriage to Althea Anna Paskewitz in August 1962 at Lucan, Redwood County, Minnesota. To this union were born, viz.: —

- Linda Sue Chellberg, born September 3, 1963
- Kenneth Ray Chellberg, born June 16, 1965
- Barbara Gwen Chellberg, born August 28, 1967
- Jennifer Chellberg, born December, 1974.
- Julie Chellberg, born October, 1977.
- Brenda Chellberg, born July, 1980.

<6> **Lois Irene Chellberg**, [p. 70] was united in marriage to Robert Jordan Burrows on September 4, 1965 at Wheaton, DuPage County, Illinois. No children.

GENERATION 7

Children of Albert Neal Diener <7>

Son of Neal Oliver and Anna Louise Diener

<7> **Sarah Marie Diener**, [p. 76] was united in marriage to Brad Walker (from San Antonio, Texas) in Chicago, Illinois.

<7> **Sharon Diener**, [p. 76] was united in marriage to Jim Seed (from St. Vincent, Minnesota) at Chicago, Illinois.

<7> **Judith Ann Diener**, [p. 76] was united in marriage to Lou Wiersum (from Maywood, Illinois) in Chicago, Illinois.

Children of Ida Louise (Bailey) Hogan <7>

Daughter of James Frederick and Leona Pearl Bailey

<7> **Stephen Earnest Hogan**, [p. 76] was united in marriage to Karol Kirk (b. June 18, 1947)on November 2, 1968. No children. They were divorced October 20, 1969.

Stephen Earnest Hogan <7> was married again to Penny Lyon Carter (b. December 6, 1957) on August 25, 1979. They were divorced on February 4, 1998. To this union one son was born, viz. : —

* Brandon Royce Hogan, born April 19, 1990.

<7> **Alfred Anthony Hogan**, [p. 76] was united in marriage to Patricia Rae Alm (b. June 29, 1950) on September 28, 1968 in Fairbanks, Alaska. To this union were born, viz.: —

* Tina Louise Hogan, born May 18, 1969.

* Alfred Anthony Hogan, Jr., born November 18, 1971.

* Stephen Curtis Lee Hogan, born April 4, 1973.

<7> **Daniel Lee Hogan**, [p. 54] was united in marriage to Jeannie Brook Williams Butler Free (b. August 3, 1958) on July 30, 1988. No children. They were divorced on February, 1992.

Children of William Frederick Bailey <7>
Son of James Frederick and Leona Pearl Bailey

<7> **Leona Pearl Bailey**, [p. 77] was united in marriage to Robert McCullock on February 11, 1967 in Los Angeles, California. To this union were born, viz.: —

- William Louis McCullock, born July 5, 1968 at New Port Beach, California.
- John Howard McCullock, born February 25, 1972 at New Port Beach, California.
- Robert James McCullock, November 4, 1974 at New Port Beach, California.

<7> **Cynthia Bailey**, [p. 77] was united in marriage to Charles Neuman on January 16, 1977 in Los Angeles, California. To this union were born, viz.: —

- Michael Charles Neuman, born November 29, 1978 in Simi Valley, California.
- Colleen Elizabeth Neuman, born July 8, 1980 in Simi Valley, California.

Children of James Delbert Kerr <7>
Son of Delbert Farlow and Lucy Mae Kerr

<7> **Victoria Lynn Kerr**, [p. 78] was united in marriage to Marcus F. Owens on May 16, 1969, no children of this union. She was divorced. On January 30, 1970 she married Daryl Edward Tippin, and to this union was born, viz.:—

- Shane Edward Tippin was born April 10, 1973.

This marriage was ended and on March 17, 1984 she married Michael Paul Vaughn, no children reported.

<7> **James Michael Kerr**, [p. 78] was united in marriage to Karen Denise Miller on November 19, 1972. She was born July 16, 1957. To this union were born, viz.:—

- Heather Lynn Kerr, born May 27, 1973.
- Christina Marie Kerr, born May 19, 1988.

Children of Earl Ebner Bailey <7>
Son of Henry Ebner Bailey and Lois Bailey

<7> **Beverly Ruth Bailey,** [p. 79] was united in marriage to Daren Lee Cox (born June 16, 1967) on April 6, 1991. To this union were born, viz. —

- Rachel Ann Cox, born July 25, 1992
- David Lee Cox, born March 22, 1997

<7> **Daniel Ebner Bailey** [p. 79] was united in marriage to Jane Elizabeth Newberry (born August 17, 1964) on November 26, 1992. To this union were born, viz. —

- Gabriel Johanna Bailey, born April 5, 1997
- Clayton Theodore Bailey, born November 29, 1998
- Eleanor Ruth Bailey, born September 22, 2002
- McAbery Daniel Bailey, born December 15, 2003

<7> **Sandra Ann Bailey** [p. 79] was united in marriage to Jeffrey Paul Nagle (born May 10, 1966) on May 6, 1993. To this union were born, viz. —

- Joshua Calvin Nagle, born August 11, 1999
- Wesley McDevitt Nagle, May 23, 2001
- Bailey Anne Nagle, May 8, 2003

Children of William Sidney Chellberg <7>

Son of William Henry and Irene G. Chellberg

<7> **Kevin John Chellberg**, [p. 79] was united in marriage to Cassia Marghezi on October 22, 1996 at Wheaton, Illinois. To this union was born, viz.: —

- Selina Lucine Chellberg, born December 2, 1997 in DuPage County, Illinois.
- Meah Sevanna Chellberg, born April 4, 2002 in DuPage County, Illinois.

<7> **Cheryl Lynn Chellberg**, [p. 79] was united in marriage to Donald L. Edyburn on May 17, 1980 at Lombard, Illinois. Divorced in 1990. To this union were born, viz.: —

- Brandon Lee Edyburn, born June 15, 1983 in DuPage County, Illinois.
- Jason David Edyburn, born January 19, 1985 in DuPage County, Illinois.

<7> **Gary Merlin Chellberg**, [p. 79] was united in marriage to Lorraine Thompson Gray on October 4, 1986 at Edinburgh, Scotland. To this union were born, viz.: —

- Samantha Lynn Chellberg, born November 19, 1988 in DuPage County, Illinois
- Lewis James Chellberg, born November 28, 1990 in DuPage County, Illinois.
- Alanna Rachel Chellberg, born June 22, 1995 in DuPage County, Illinois.
- Vivian Elyssa Chellberg, born November 3, 1997 in DuPage County, Illinois.
- Elaine Louise Chellberg, born April 30, 1999 in DuPage County, Illinois.
- Bradley William Chellberg, born September 1, 2002 in DuPage County, Illinois.

Children of Donna Sue (Chellberg) Paskewitz <7>
Daughter of William Henry and Irene G. Chellberg

<7> **Ronald Dean Paskewitz**, [p. 79] was united in marriage to Naomi Tuffin (of Southampton, England) in Southampton, England.

<7> **Sandra Kay Paskewitz**, [p. 79] was united in marriage to Dick Waskey (of Washington, D.C.) in Vesta, Minnesota.

<7> **Beverly Sue Paskewitz**, [p. 79] was united in marriage to Charles Schmidt (of Chicago) in Vesta, Minnesota. They live in Indianapolis, Indiana.

<7> **Rebecca Paskewitz**, [p. 79] was united in marriage to Steve Carpani (of Tillsonburg, Ontario, Canada) in Vesta, Minnesota.

Children of Thomas Ebner Chellberg <7>
Son of William Henry and Irene G. Chellberg

<7> **Linda Sue Chellberg**, [p. 80] was united in marriage to Greg Markham. They live in Los Angeles. To this union were born:
- Jennifer Markham, b. October 1982
- Beverly Markham, b. July 1984
- Cheryl Markham, b. April 1986
- Chuck Markham, b. September 1990

<7> **Kenneth Ray Chellberg**, [p. 80] was united in marriage to Joyce Ann Druckenmiller (of Westfield, New Jersey). They are now divorced. Joyce Ann lives in the Minneapolis, Minnesota area. To this union were born:

- Kurt Chellberg, b. February 1985
- Vern Chellberg, b. November 1986

- Glenn Chellberg, b. September, 1988

Kenneth R Chellberg was married again to Barbara L (?) and moved to Woodstock, McHenry, Illinois. Kenneth died May 8, 2013. To this union were born:

- Shelby Chellberg
- Kenzie Chellberg (twin)
- Haley Chellberg (twin)

<7> **Barbara Gwen Chellberg**, [p. 80] was united in marriage to Jeff Lock (of Westfield, New Jersey).

GENERATION 8

Children of Alfred Anthony Hogan <8>
Son of Anthony Hogan and Ida Louise Bailey

<8> **Tina Louise Hogan**, [p. 83] was united in marriage to Donald George Haislet III on November 26, 1994. To this union two children were born, viz.: —

* Raeann Taylor Haislet, born February 13, 1997.
* Mackenzie Haislet, born July 18, 1999.

<8> **Alfred Anthony Hogan Jr.**, [p. 83] was united in marriage to Julie Anna Plemons (b. January 11, 1972) on June 28, 1993. To this union were born two children, viz.: —

* Zerek Anthony Hogan, born February 14, 1995.
* Zackery David Hogan, born April 24, 1996.

<8> **Stephen Curtis Lee Hogan**, [p. 83] was united in marriage to Debra Maybelle Henson (b. April 14, 1971) on May 11, 1996. To this union two children were born, viz.: —

* Hunter Lee Hogan, born September 24, 1996.
* Kyler Blake Hogan, born March 2, 2001.

Children of Victoria Lynn (Kerr) Tippin <8>
Daughter of James Delbert and Norma Lou Kerr

<8> **Shane Edward Tippin**, [p. 84] was married to Nicole B. Ferris on August 4, 1979, to this union was born one son, viz.:

* Raylor Dean Tippin, born June 26, 1997

Children of James Michael Kerr <8>
Son of James Delbert and Norma Lou Kerr

<8> **Heather Lynn Kerr**, [p. 85] was married to Steven James Cain on November 14, 1991, to this union was born two children, viz.: —
- Teresa Rene Cain, born October 7, 1993
- Kevin Andrew Cain, February 26, 1997

Children of Darin Lee Cox and Beverly Ruth Cox <8>
Daughter of Earl Ebner Bailey and Ruth Ann Bailey

<8> **Rachel Ann Cox**, [p. 85] was married to Nathan New-comer (born April 12, 1992) on September 13, 2020. No children.

Children of Kevin J. Chellberg and Cassia Chellberg <8>
Son oof William S. Chellberg and Doris Jean Paskewitz

<8> **Selina Lousine Chellberg,** (p. 85) was married to Joshua Zowolski on June 23, 2019 in Aurora, Illinois. To this union there are no children.

Children of Gary M. Chellberg and Lorraine Chellberg <8>
Son of William S. Chellberg and Doris Jean Paskewitz

<8> **Lewis James Chellberg**, [p. 85] was married to Lauren Klassen on September 5, 2016 in Pocatello, Idaho. To this union was born one child, viz.: --
- Kelsey Kay Chellberg, born April 2, 2020.

<8> **Alanna Rachel Chellberg**, [p. 85] was married to Alistair Henry (of Glasgow, Scotlnd) on June 29,2015 at Wheaton, Illinois. To this union there are no children.

INDEX OF NAMES

Adler	Clarence Earnest	54
Adler	Ethel Delphine	54
Adler	Frayne Chilton	54
Adler	George Alberts	54
Adler	George E.	54
Adler	Nellie May	54
Adler	Raymond LeRoy	54
Allison	Alice	38
Alm	Patricia Rae	83
Anderson	Elfie	54
Atikson	Alma Lucille	74
Atikson	Earnest Tyler	52, 74
Atikson	Gilma Juel	74
Atikson	Jennie	52, 75
Atikson	Katherine May	74
Atikson	Loren Russell	74
Atikson	Rena Orline	74
Atikson	Roland Ernest	74
Atikson	William	52
Avery	Mary H.	39
Ayres	Maude	51
Babb	Amanda	39
Bailey	Abraham	17
Bailey	Absalom	17, 25
Bailey	Alvin L.	24, 39
Bailey	American Ann	21, 29
Bailey	Anna Hazel	44
Bailey	Anna Louise	44, 68
Bailey	Artie M.	35, 58
Bailey	Barbary	13
Bailey	Bertha Lucille	68, 77
Bailey	Beverly Ruth	79
Bailey	Buford E.	58

Bailey	Burnelle	66
Bailey	Catherine	17
Bailey	Charles C.	25, 44
Bailey	Clarence E.	37
Bailey	Clarence W.	39
Bailey	Clayton Theodore	85
Bailey	Clifford	36
Bailey	Clyde Ugene	61
Bailey	Curtis LeRoy	52
Bailey	Cynthia	77, 84
Bailey	Daniel Ebner	79
Bailey	Daniel V.	24, 40
Bailey	Daniel V. (2)	66
Bailey	Danine Joan	78
Bailey	Darren James	78
Bailey	David	31, 52
Bailey	Dean Heacock	49
Bailey	Deana W.	36, 60
Bailey	DeLoris Bailey	66
Bailey	Denise Elaine	78
Bailey	Derrick Edward	77
Bailey	Dessie Aileen	44, 68
Bailey	Dessie M.	25, 44
Bailey	Dolly May	44
Bailey	Dora	50
Bailey	Earl E.	58
Bailey	Earl Ebner	69, 78
Bailey	Edgar S.	23, 37
Bailey `	Edith E.	30, 50
Bailey	Eleanor Ruth	85
Bailey	Elizabeth	13, 18
Bailey	Elizabeth (2)	17, 24
Bailey	Elizabeth (3)	21, 29

Bailey . . . . Elizabeth (4) 22, 34
Bailey . . . . Ernest 39
Bailey . . . . Esther E. 66
Bailey . . . . Eva Ann 22, 34
Bailey . . . . Fannie J. 35, 59
Bailey . . . . Fernando Francis 51
Bailey . . . . Fernando Wood 21, 30
Bailey . . . . Frank P. 31, 51
Bailey . . . . Frank William 51
Bailey . . . . Fred 30, 51
Bailey . . . . Gabriel Johanna 85
Bailey . . . . George 18, 25
Bailey . . . . George (2) 32, 52
Bailey . . . . George W. 23, 35
Bailey . . . . Gertha M. 37, 62
Bailey . . . . Glen C. 36
Bailey . . . . Glen R. 37
Bailey . . . . Golda Alice 30, 49
Bailey . . . . Goldie V. 35, 58
Bailey . . . . Grace 32, 52
Bailey . . . . Grover L. 35, 59
Bailey . . . . Harold Wesley 40, 66
Bailey . . . . Harry E. 35, 58
Bailey . . . . Harry E.(2) 66
Bailey . . . . Harry Edward 40,66
Bailey . . . . Harry M. 31
Bailey . . . . Hasson E. 25, 43
Bailey . . . . Heail R. 29, 49
Bailey . . . . Helen M. 49
Bailey . . . . Henry 17, 25
Bailey . . . . Henry Ebner 45, 69
Bailey . . . . Ida Louise 68, 76
Bailey . . . . Irene 50

Bailey . . . . Irene Gertrude 45, 69
Bailey . . . . Isaac 17
Bailey . . . . J. Orvil 37, 61
Bailey . . . . Jack Edward 49
Bailey . . . . Jacob 13
Bailey . . . . James Carl 78
Bailey . . . . James Curtis 21, 31
Bailey . . . . James Frederick 44, 68
Bailey . . . . James Oday 30, 50
Bailey . . . . James Robert 69, 77
Bailey . . . . James W. 25, 44
Bailey . . . . Jefferson D. 30, 49
Bailey . . . . Joan J. 66
Bailey . . . . Joan 69, 77
Bailey . . . . John 13
Bailey . . . . John (2) 17, 22
Bailey . . . . John H. 25
Bailey . . . . John P. 21, 29
Bailey . . . . John T. 23, 37
Bailey . . . . Joseph Wright 21, 30
Bailey . . . . Kathleen J. 37
Bailey . . . . Katie Ann 21, 29
Bailey . . . . Kenneth R. 58
Bailey . . . . Laura 21, 30
Bailey . . . . Lena G. 30, 50
Bailey . . . . Leona Pearl 77, 84
Bailey . . . . Lesla 40, 65
Bailey . . . . Lidia 13
Bailey . . . . Lidia (2) 17, 24
Bailey . . . . Lola G. 25, 45
Bailey . . . . Louis A. 24, 40
Bailey . . . . Loyd D. 30, 51
Bailey . . . . Lucy May 45, 69

Bailey . . . . Luna A. 35, 58
Bailey . . . . Lydia 51
Bailey . . . . Lyle Bright 51
Bailey . . . . Lynette Michelle 78
Bailey . . . . Margary M. 37
Bailey . . . . Marion 22, 34
Bailey . . . . Martha J. 36
Bailey . . . . Marthia 17
Bailey . . . . Mary 31, 52
Bailey . . . . Mary Ann 17, 23
Bailey . . . . Mary E. 25
Bailey . . . . Mary M. 23, 35
Bailey . . . . Mary Margaret 69, 77
Bailey . . . . McAbery Daniel 85
Bailey . . . . Mildred Lenore 44
Bailey . . . . Minnie B. 25
Bailey . . . . Molly 13
Bailey . . . . Nancy 13
Bailey . . . . Nellie 21, 31
Bailey . . . . Nettie 23, 36
Bailey . . . . Nicholas 13
Bailey . . . . Nicholas (2) 17, 21
Bailey . . . . Nicholas (3) 31
Bailey . . . . Nora 23, 37
Bailey . . . . Norma Aline 52
Bailey . . . . Norval 66
Bailey . . . . Olga Jesse 35
Bailey . . . . Opal C. 36
Bailey . . . . Peter 13, 17
Bailey . . . . Peter J. 17, 23
Bailey . . . . Peter N. 23, 36
Bailey . . . . Philip 13
Bailey . . . . Richard Wayne 58

Bailey . . . . James Robert 69, 77
Bailey . . . . Ronold Marion 58
Bailey . . . . Ruby G. 58
Bailey . . . . Russell 31
Bailey . . . . Ruth Irene 69, 79
Bailey . . . . Sandra Ann 79
Bailey . . . . Sarah 22
Bailey . . . . Sarah E. 30, 49
Bailey . . . . Sarah Elizabeth 51
Bailey . . . . Shirley Sue 69
Bailey . . . . Solome 18, 25
Bailey . . . . Susan 17, 21
Bailey . . . . Susan E. 23, 36
Bailey . . . . Theodore 32
Bailey . . . . Van P. 21, 31
Bailey . . . . Vileta 58
Bailey . . . . Viora Caroline 58
Bailey . . . . Virginia May 52
Bailey . . . . Virginia Pauline Bome 51
Bailey . . . . Walter 30, 50
Bailey . . . . Warren D. 21, 31
Bailey . . . . Willard Absalom 44
Bailey . . . . William Edgar 36, 60
Bailey . . . . William Frederick 68, 77
Bailey . . . . Willie 23
Barber . . . . Allen Lee 77
Barber . . . . Brian David 77
Barber . . . . David 77
Baun . . . . Sarah 68
Bogerman . . . . Charles Clifford 68
Bogerman . . . . Clifford 68
Bogerman . . . . Ruth Elizabeth 68
Boland . . . . Helen E. 49

Booth	John	73
Booth	John (Jr.)	73
Britton	Art	29,48
Britton	Franklin D.	48
Britton	George	29
Britton	George (2)	48
Britton	Georgia	29
Britton	Mahala A.	29, 48
Britton	Ruth J.	48
Britton	Sadie E.	29, 48
Brock	Lula	50
Brown	Blanche	56
Brown	Dora M.	58
Brown	Ethel	56
Brown	Harry C.	64
Brown	Ruth Ann	78
Bruner	Alice Carrie	64
Buchanan	John M.	40
Burrows	Robert Jordan	80
Bush	Ardrie L. (see note p.75)	56
Bush	Louis A.	75
Bush	Paul A.	75
Bush	Tilman	56
Bush	Tilman W.	75
Cain	Kevin Andrew	91
Cain	Steven James	91
Cain	Teresa Rene	91
Caldwell	Ara C.	54
Campbell	Delbert E.	56
Campbell	Edith G.	56
Campbell	Elvin E.	57
Campbell	Eva A.	34, 57
Campbell	Eva Alma	56

Campbell . . . . Everett W. 57
Campbell . . . . Frances B. 56
Campbell . . . . Gearld E. 57
Campbell . . . . Geneva V. 57
Campbell . . . . Harold E. 57
Campbell . . . . James M. 34, 57
Campbell . . . . John L. 34, 56
Campbell . . . . Juanita L. 56
Campbell . . . . Kenneth B. 56
Campbell . . . . Martin 34
Campbell . . . . Martin O. 34, 56
Campbell ` . . . . Mary C. 34, 56
Campbell ` . . . . Minerva 22
Campbell ` . . . . Oliver D. 34, 56
Campbell . . . . `Oris M. 57
Campbell . . . . Rosalee 34
Campbell . . . . Ruth G. 57
Campbell . . . . Sarah E. 34, 57
Campbell . . . . Tessie O. 34
Campbell . . . . Trilby M. 56
Carpani . . . . Steven James 87
Carter . . . . Penny Lyon 83
Center . . . . George (Jr.) 75
Center . . . . George M. 75
Chellberg . . . . Alanna Rachel 86, 91
Chellberg . . . . Barbara Gwen 80, 88
Chellberg . . . . Barbara L 88
Chellberg . . . . Bradley William 86
Chellberg . . . . Brenda 80
Chellberg . . . . Cheryl Lynn 79, 86
Chellberg . . . . Donna Sue 70, 79
Chellberg . . . . Elaine Louise 86
Chellberg . . . . Gary Merlin 79, 85

Chellberg . . . . Glenn 88
Chellberg . . . . Haley 88
Chellberg . . . . Jennifer 80
Chellberg . . . . Julie 80
Chellberg . . . . Karen May 76
Chellberg . . . . Kelsey Kay 91
Chellberg . . . . Kenneth Ray 80, 88
Chellberg . . . . Kenzie 88
Chellberg . . . . Kevin John 79, 86
Chellberg . . . . Kurt 88
Chellberg . . . . Lewis James 86, 91
Chellberg . . . . Linda Sue 80, 87
Chellberg . . . . Lois Irene 70, 80
Chellberg . . . . Meah Sevanna 86
Chellberg . . . . Samantha Lynn 86
Chellberg . . . . Selina Lousine 86, 91
Chellberg . . . . Shelby 88
Chellberg . . . . Thomas Ebner 70, 80
Chellberg . . . . Vern 88
Chellberg . . . . Vivian Elyssa 86
Chellberg . . . . William Henry 69
Chellberg . . . . William Sidney 70, 79
Cherry . . . . Claud 65
Cherry . . . . Maud M. 65
Cherry . . . . Rita Fern 65
Clark . . . . Homer 74
Coen . . . . Eva Jane 53
Collens . . . . Irine 73
Collier . . . . Elizabeth 64
Collier . . . . Ernest C. 64
Collier . . . . John W. 64
Collier . . . . Martha 18
Conner . . . . Treca 65

Coombs . . . . Nora E. 58
Copeland . . . . Lois A. 57
Cox . . . . Daren Lee 85
Cox . . . . Rachel Ann 85, 91
Cox . . . . David Lee 85
Creed . . . . Amanda A. 25
Crumrine . . . . Samuel 26
Dale . . . . Charles B. 35, 59
Dale . . . . Esther 77
Dale . . . . Herbert S. 59
Dale . . . . Ira O. 35, 59
Dale . . . . John H. 35
Dale . . . . Lilly A. 33
Dale . . . . Lola D. 35
Dale . . . . Marian June 59
Dale . . . . Susie Fern 59
Dale . . . . W. Edgar 35, 59
Dale . . . . William C. 59
Davidson . . . . Anna May 39
Deatley . . . . Ellen 33
Dennison . . . . Pleasant 50
Dennison . . . . Richard Bailey 51
Diener . . . . Albert Neal 68, 76
Diener . . . . Diane 76
Diener . . . . Ella Marie 68, 76
Diener . . . . James Albert 76
Diener . . . . Judith Ann 76, 83
Diener . . . . Michael 76
Diener . . . . Neal Oliver 68
Diener . . . . Roy 76
Diener . . . . Sarah Marie 76, 83
Diener . . . . Sharon 76, 83
Dobson . . . . Edith Bell 74

Doeset . . . . Clara 66
Doran . . . . Edith 51
Drager . . . . Ida Elizabeth 64
Druckenmiller . . . . Joyce Ann 88
Drummond . . . . Christine Luella 43
Drummond . . . . Evalyn Lidia 43
Drummond . . . . James Harrison 43
Drummond . . . . John William 43
Drummond . . . . Thomas Henry 43
Drummond . . . . William Leonard 43
Duncan . . . . Vaughn 59
Eaglin . . . . Mary 51
Eckert . . . . Margaret C. 29
Edyburn . . . . Brandon Lee 86
Edyburn . . . . Donald Lee 86
Edyburn . . . . Jason David 86
Eggers . . . . Della 59
Ellern . . . . Ella N. 53
Emday . . . . Catherine 22
Estborn . . . . Dortha Jane 52
Estborn . . . . Paul 52
Estell . . . . Alfred 63
Estell . . . . Virginia M. 63
Favor . . . . (unknown)? 26
Favor . . . . Frances 26
Favor . . . . Jake 26
Favor . . . . John 26
Favor . . . . Peter 26
Favor . . . . William 26
Feaster . . . . Phoebe Ann 23
Ferris . . . . Nicole B. 90
Free . . . . Jeannie B. W. B. 84
Freeland . . . . Grace 75

Gibson	Lora E.	37
Golding	Charles W.	48
Golding	Charles W. (2)	73
Golding	Elizabeth A.	48, 74
Golding	Estella R.	48, 74
Golding	Esther Q.	48, 74
Golding	George E.	48, 73
Golding	Grace E.	48, 73
Golding	Mildred J.	73
Gray	Lillie Mirtle	64
Gray	Lorraine Thompson	86
Grimmes	Pearl	56
Grote	Donald A.	74
Grote	Frank E.	74
Grote	Laurence	74
Grote	Margaret E.	74
Haislet	Donald George III	90
Haislet	Raeann Taylor	90
Haislet	Mackenzie	90
Hall	Bernice M.	36, 60
Hall	Clara L.	36
Hall	Elizabeth	32
Hall	Marvan	36, 60
Hall	Robert T.	36
Halterman	Mary Ellen Creed	21
Hamilton	Charles M.	49
Hamilton	Delta E.	49
Hamilton	Golda M.	49, 74
Hamilton	Leta Kathryn	49
Hamilton	Raymond T.	49
Hamilton	Wanita E.	49
Hamlock	Minnie	61
Harrison	Pauline	55

Hart . . . . .Ora A. 53
Haus . . . . .Edward 52
Haus . . . . .Frank Edward 52
Hazlett . . . . .Cecil C. 56
Hazlett . . . . .Harold Dale 55
Hazlett . . . . .J.J. 55
Heacock . . . . .Julia B. 49
Hedge . . . . .Audry 37
Hedge . . . . .Doris 37
Hedge . . . . .Floyd 37
Hedge . . . . .Gladys 37, 61
Hedge . . . . .Harvey 36
Henderson . . . . .Edward F. 50
Henderson . . . . .Fay 50
Henderson . . . . .Joseph 24
Henderson . . . . .Lucinda 24, 40
Hendricks . . . . .Maggie 67
Henry . . . . .Alistair 91
Henson . . . . .Charles C. 42
Henson . . . . .Clarence U. 41, 67
Henson . . . . .Clyde W. 41
Henson . . . . .Debra Maybelle 90
Henson . . . . .Edna Alberta 67
Henson . . . . .Ethel A. 41
Henson . . . . .George B. 41
Henson . . . . .Jennie F. 67
Henson . . . . .Leona L. 42
Henson . . . . .Lilly H. 42
Henson . . . . .Ola G. 41
Henton . . . . .Jennettea 51
Hocker . . . . .Alva 59
Hocker . . . . .Keith B. 59
Hogan . . . . .Alfred 76

Hogan	Alfred Anthony	76, 83
Hogan	Alfred Anthony Jr	83
Hogan	Brandon Royce	83
Hogan	Cecil	63
Hogan	Daniel Lee	76, 84
Hogan	Hunter Lee	90
Hogan	Kyler Blake	90
Hogan	Stephen E.	76, 83
Hogan	Stephen Curtis Lee	83
Hogan	Tina Louise	83
Hogan	Zackery David	90
Hogan	Zerek Anthony	90
Holland	Leola	66
Howe	Beatrice Arletta	63
Howe	James R.	63
Howe	Lola Marie	63
Hudson	Oka May	37
Humfleet	John	76
Isley	Sarah Ann (N.?)	21
Jakay	Henry	75
Jakay	Hoener T.	75
Jakay	Pauline W.	75
Jakay	Samuel W.	75
Jakay	Sidney A.	75
Jones	Leona Pearl	68
Keeney	Ruth Ann	58
Kerr	Byron Dean	78
Kerr	Christina Marie	85
Kerr	Delbert Farlow	69
Kerr	Heather Lynn	85
Kerr	James Delbert	69, 78
Kerr	James Michael	78, 85
Kerr	Mary Jean	69, 78

Kerr	Victoria Lynn	78, 84
Killon	E.W.	53
Killon	Lyle L.	53
Kirk	Karol	83
Klassen	Lauren	91
Kolkusler	Mary	31
Kurr	Edward	22
Leak	Ethan A.	36
Leak	John Mac	60
Leak	Lyal	36, 60
Leak	Richard L.	60
Leak	Sarah E.	59
Lee	Edith E.	37, 61
Lee	Jessie Myrtle	37, 61
Lee	John W.	37
Lee	Lewana	61
Lee	Otis Russell	37, 61
Lee	Ruby Grace	37
Lee	Rue B.	37
Leffler	C. Cassie	25
Leffler	Susanna	13
Lingenfelter	Clyde	63
Lock	Jeff	88
Loutzl	Margaret	73
Lowe	Nancy Elizabeth	44
Lucas	Carl (Jr.)	77
Lucas	Dawn Janine	77
Lucas	Gary Phillip	77
Mames	Eva	67
Marghezi	Cassia	86
Markham	Greg	87
Martin	Elizabeth Hall	25
Martin	Eva L.	43

Mason	Ben	.26
Mason	Benjamin	.26
Mason	John	.26
Mason	Sarah	.26
Mason	William	.26
McAbery	Lois	.69
McCain	Absalom	.23
McCain	Aletha Cherry	.65
McCain	Alice R.	.62
McCain	Alonzo Fay	.38, 64
McCain	Cecil Gordon	.39, 65
McCain	Charles F.	.38, 62
McCain	Charles Herbert	.64
McCain	Edith Faye	.64
McCain	Elmer Howard	.38, 64
McCain	Eva	.62
McCain	Flossie Pearl	.38, 63
McCain	Franklin Paul	.39, 65
McCain	George Bertram	.38, 64
McCain	George Raymond	.64
McCain	George Washington	.23, 38
McCain	Gradie Fern	.39, 65
McCain	Grady Ruth	.62
McCain	Jesse Clarence	.39, 65
McCain	John Franklin	.23, 39
McCain	John W.	.62
McCain	Justin Frances	.65
McCain	Lulu	.38, 62
McCain	Margarette Elizabeth	.23, 38
McCain	Marjorie Lucille	.64
McCain	Mary Alice	.62
McCain	Merrill M.	.65
McCain	Rena	62

McCain . . . . Ruth Maxine 64
McCain . . . . Sabina Jane 23, 39
McCain . . . . Wallace 38, 62
McCain . . . . Wanetta Fern 65
McCain . . . . William Frederick 62
McCain . . . . William Solomon 23, 38
McCullock . . . . John Howard 84
McCullock . . . . Robert 84
McCullock . . . . Robert James 84
McCullock . . . . William Louis 84
McDonald . . . . Ivy 54
McHugh . . . . Beatrice R. 66
McKenzie . . . . Edna 67
McKenzie . . . . Grover 67
Mertz . . . . Mary (Isham) 69
Miller . . . . Bernice 73
Miller . . . . Bob 65
Miller . . . . Clinton B. 61
Miller . . . . Edson 65
Miller . . . . Edward 65
Miller . . . . Jessie Lawrence 61
Miller . . . . Karen Denise 85
Miller . . . . Maryland 65
Mings . . . . John 39
Mings . . . . Maud 39, 64
Mings . . . . Stacy 39, 64
Mosley . . . . Lou 42
Mount . . . . Flo 50
Nagle . . . . Jeffrey Paul 85
Nagle . . . . Joshua Calvin 85
Nagle . . . . Wesley McDivitt 85
Nagle . . . . Bailey Anne 85
Nash . . . . Alfred LeRoy 63

Nash	Emma Francis	38, 63
Nash	Esther Ethel	38, 63
Nash	George W.	38, 63
Nash	George William	63
Nash	John	38
Nash	Lucinda May	63
Nash	Scott Ray	63
Nash	Walter Clyde	63
Nash	William	38, 63
Neuman	Charles	84
Neuman	Colleen Elizabeth	84
Neuman	Michael Charles	84
Newberry	Jane Elizabeth	85
Newcomer	Nathan	91
Noah	Fay F.	50
Noah	Opal S.	50
Noah	Orvil P.	50
Noah	Ruthe L.	50
Nothern	Francis Harland	51
Nothern	Roy	51
Nothern	William Oliver	51
Offitt	Florenzo	42
Offitt	Frederick George	42
Offitt	Leo Thomas	42
Offitt	O. C.	42
Offitt	Oliver Charles	42
Offitt	Olonzo	42
Offitt	Walter Floyd	42
Omard	Elizabeth	67
Owens	John	76
Owens	Lori Ann	76
Owens	Marcus F.	84
Parker	Alice L.	62

Parker . . . . Jessie M. 62
Parker . . . . Maurice 62
Parker . . . . Robert 62
Paskewitz . . . . Althea Anna 80
Paskewitz . . . . Beverly Sue 79, 87
Paskewitz . . . . Doris Jean 79
Paskewitz . . . . Lloyd 79
Paskewitz . . . . Lori Ann 79
Paskewitz . . . . Rebecca 79, 87
Paskewitz . . . . Ronald Dean 79, 87
Paskewitz . . . . Sandra Kay 79, 87
Paskewitz . . . . Tim 79
Pearce . . . . Amanda Alice 22
Pearce . . . . Amy Leona 34, 56
Pearce . . . . Arie Beaughn 33, 55
Pearce . . . . Blythe Valentine 45
Pearce . . . . Burnell Leslie 55
Pearce . . . . Cecil V. 32, 53
Pearce . . . . Charles D. 32, 53
Pearce . . . . Charles M. 22, 33
Pearce . . . . Claud A. 53
Pearce . . . . Claud F. 32, 52
Pearce . . . . Coralie Helen 75
Pearce . . . . D. W. 45
Pearce . . . . Dora A. 32
Pearce . . . . Eliza Jane 22, 32
Pearce . . . . Estelle F. 32, 52
Pearce . . . . Genevia Adaline 55
Pearce . . . . George 33
Pearce . . . . George Thomas 22, 33
Pearce . . . . John Willis 22, 33
Pearce . . . . Leora E. 53
Pearce . . . . Mary Edna 22, 32

Pearce . . . . Mary J. 32, 53
Pearce . . . . Maud P. 32
Pearce . . . . Morris F. 32
Pearce . . . . Nellie D. 32, 53
Pearce . . . . Ornetta L. 22
Pearce . . . . Paul F. 53
Pearce . . . . Rossell J. 22
Pearce . . . . Sarah 33
Pearce . . . . Tessie Maud 33, 54
Pearce . . . . Tiny Blossom 53
Pearce . . . . Vella Maud 33, 55
Pearce . . . . Vera May 33, 55
Pearce . . . . William A. 22, 32
Pearce . . . . William Leslie 33, 55
Pearce . . . . Wilma Lucille 45
Pearce . . . . Zella M. 53, 75
Pearce . . . . Zulla F. 53, 75
Pearcy . . . . Laura 33
Pearson . . . . Maud W. 40
Pebble . . . . Daisy Iowa 55
Pebble . . . . Eva M. 55
Pebble . . . . John 54
Philips . . . . Margaret 62
Pickett . . . . Norma Lou 78
Plemons . . . . Julie Anna 90
Power . . . . Emmett E. 57
Power . . . . Helen M. 57
Power . . . . Vernal E. 57
Power . . . . Victor E. 57
Pratt . . . . Carl R. 57
Pratt . . . . Phillip 57
Pratt . . . . William M. 57
Pritchett . . . . Andrew S. 58

Pritchett . . . . Charles E. 58
Pritchett . . . . Jewell B. 58
Pritchett . . . . Lowell E. 58
Pritchett . . . . Ruby T. 58
Ragsdale . . . . Vida E. 60
Randal . . . . Elsie L. 61
Ratcliff . . . . Oral Hall 60
Ratcliff . . . . Robert 60
Ray . . . . Estle D. 62
Redenbough . . . . Ella C. 31
Reed . . . . Berbel 51
Reed . . . . Conrad 18
Reed . . . . Dan 18
Reed . . . . Eliza 18, 26
Reed . . . . Jacob 18
Reed . . . . Jake 18
Reed . . . . Lidia 18, 26
Reed . . . . Mary 18
Reed . . . . Rebecca J. 22
Reed . . . . Sarah P. 31
Reeves . . . . Halsey 74
Reser . . . . Blanche E. 48
Reser . . . . Charles H. 48, 73
Reser . . . . Ebert M. 48, 73
Reser . . . . Eveline 48
Reser . . . . Irene 48
Reser . . . . Lawrence 73
Reser . . . . Melvin E. 48
Reser . . . . Orvilla 48, 73
Righer . . . . Lilly M. 31
Riser . . . . Grace 62
Roberts . . . . Cassie E. 44
Roberts . . . . Maggie Alma 48

Roberts . . . . William E. 44
Robertson . . . . Marjorie 77
Roebuck . . . . Bessie Ray 43
Roebuck . . . . Charles F. 24
Roebuck . . . . Derias P. 24
Roebuck . . . . Dolly Tawell 43
Roebuck . . . . Elsie May 41
Roebuck . . . . Emma L. 24, 41
Roebuck . . . . Ethel Bell 43
Roebuck . . . . Frances Marion ` 24, 42
Roebuck . . . . Francis Edward 43
Roebuck . . . . George (Jr.?) 41
Roebuck . . . . George B. McCleen 24
Roebuck . . . . Henry 41
Roebuck . . . . Hiram A. 24
Roebuck . . . . Jack 41
Roebuck . . . . James Ebbon 43
Roebuck . . . . James W. 41, 67
Roebuck . . . . Jennie Pearl 43
Roebuck . . . . Johannie Sylvester 43
Roebuck . . . . John Grover 42, 68
Roebuck . . . . John H. N. 24, 41
Roebuck . . . . John L. 41, 67
Roebuck . . . . Laura 41
Roebuck . . . . Lillie 24, 43
Roebuck . . . . Lilly Emily 43
Roebuck . . . . Lola Irene 43
Roebuck . . . . Lola R. 41
Roebuck . . . . Louis 41
Roebuck . . . . Marie 41, 67
Roebuck . . . . Mary E. 24, 42
Roebuck . . . . Robert E. L. 24
Roebuck . . . . Rose Ann 43

Roebuck . . . . Sadie Marie 43
Roebuck . . . . Sarah 41
Roebuck . . . . Seargie Lee 43
Roebuck . . . . Thomas J. 24
Roebuck . . . . Thomas Benton 24, 42
Roebuck . . . . Truman K. 41
Rose . . . . Edith 60
Salb . . . . Bettie J. 61
Salb . . . . George L. 61
Salb . . . . Madeline G. 61
Salb . . . . Margaret M. 61
Salb . . . . Maxine T. 61
Schmidt . . . . Charles 87
Schuberth . . . . James Timothy 77
Schuberth . . . . LaVern 77
Schuberth . . . . Thomas Frederick 77
Scott . . . . Clara 60
Seed . . . . Jim 83
Sinks . . . . John LeRoy 61
Sinks . . . . Roy E. 61
Sipe . . . . Margaret 52
Smith . . . . A. E. 31
Smith . . . . David 34
Smith . . . . Forest E. 31, 51
Smith . . . . Josephine 41
Smith . . . . Mary A. 31, 51
Smith . . . . Oral N. 31, 51
Smith . . . . Theron P. 75
Smith . . . . William E. 31
Souders . . . . Eva May 49
Souders . . . . James 49
Souders . . . . Lucy May 49
Stanbrook . . . . Elizabeth 17

Stevens . . . . Alice L. 40
Stickford . . . . Ida Sophia Louise 44
Summers . . . . Ede Merl 73
Summers . . . . Ermatine J. 73
Summers . . . . John T. 73
Summers . . . . John V. 73
Summers . . . . Ruth 73
Sweeney . . . . Jesse 32
Taylor . . . . Floyd B. 53
Templeton . . . . David F. 30
Templeton . . . . Leona M. 30, 50
Templeton . . . . Nannie 30
Tevis . . . . Fannie 30
Thomas . . . . John Milton 78
Thomas . . . . Mark 78
Thomas . . . . Marsha 78
Thomas . . . . Melanie 78
Thomas . . . . Melinda 78
Tippin . . . . Daryl Edward 84
Tippin . . . . Raylor Dean 90
Tippin . . . . Shane Edward 84, 90
Townsend . . . . Sarah A. 25
Tramwell . . . . Donnie 59
Trip . . . . Dessie May 43
Truitt . . . . Ada Frances 67
Truitt . . . . Edward 67
Truitt . . . . Ida Alice 40
Truitt . . . . Isaac A. (Jr.) 40
Truitt . . . . Isaac D. 40
Truitt . . . . James B. 40, 66
Truitt . . . . James Frances 67
Truitt . . . . Margaret Elizabeth 67
Truitt . . . . Mary Eva 40

Truitt . . . . Nadine Alice 66
Truitt . . . . Ora Alice 66
Truitt . . . . Walter M. 40, 66
Truitt . . . . Warren L. 40, 67
Truitt . . . . Warren Lee 67
Tucker . . . . Benjamin 29
Tucker . . . . Ebert 29
Tucker . . . . Molly 29
Tucker . . . . William 29
Tuffin . . . . Naomi 87
Vaughn . . . . Michael Paul 84
Vest . . . . Hattie F. 35
Wahl . . . . Martha L. 65
Waldon . . . . Zola 67
Walker . . . . Brad 83
Walker . . . . Frances M. 52
Waskey . . . . Dick 87
Watson . . . . Robert O. 32
West E. . . . . Lilly 39
West . . . . Fannie M. 38
Whitzel . . . . Arthur 55
Whitzel . . . . Paul Pearce 55
Widner . . . . David 29
Wiersum . . . . Louis 83
Wilkert . . . . Edward L. 74
Wills . . . . Lavina A. 60
Wills . . . . Nellie B. 60
Wills . . . . Orvil 60
Wilson . . . . Clara Francis 44
Woodard . . . . Bert G. 55
Woodard . . . . Irving Clyde 33, 54
Woodard . . . . Lanford Donald 54
Woodard . . . . Mona Andry 54

Woodard . . . . Nelly Esther 33, 54
Woodard . . . . Raymond Thurman . . . 33, 54
Woodard . . . . Viola May 33, 54
Woodard . . . . Willa Wyvitte 54
Woodard . . . . William C. 33
Worland . . . . Margaret (Hicks) 69
Wyatt . . . . Robert E. 55
Wyatt . . . . Robert E. (Jr.) 55
Young . . . . Rachel C. 34
Zowolski . . . . Joshua 91

Family Notes

Family Notes

Family Notes

Family Notes